RUTHLESS PUTTING

MIKE SOUTHERN

an imprint of Defiant Publishing LLC

Ruthless Putting
©2009 Mike Southern

Cover design by Mike Southern
Book design by Mike Southern

All rights reserved.

No part of this publication may be reproduced in any form or by any electronic or mechanical means including information storage and retrieval systems, without permission in writing from the author. The only exception is by a reviewer, who may quote short excerpts in a review. Short quotations from other works are used in this book; they are included only to ensure the accuracy of what is said, and are protected by their own respective copyrights.

Published by Defiant Books, an imprint of
Defiant Publishing LLC
www.defiantpub.com

Printed in the USA and abroad by Lightning Source Inc.
www.lightningsource.com

First published in June 2009

ISBN-13: 978-0-9815581-1-0
ISBN-10: 0-9815581-1-9

Table of Contents

Introduction:
    Ruthlessness is Its Own Reward 9

1
    The Mind of the Ruthless Putter 15

2
    The Basic Principles of Good Putting 20

3
    The Universal Move 25

4
    Meet the Four Basic Strokes 32

5
    The Shrug Stroke 39

6
    The Hug Stroke. 43

7
    The Fold Stroke 48

8
    The Pop Stroke. 53

9
    Why Your Grip Matters 60

10
    The Gravity of the Situation. 71

11
    Why Can't I Aim? 82

12
    Fine-Tuning Your Putter .94

13
    Kiss Your Yips Goodbye. 104

14
    Putting It All Together. 120

Appendix:
    Troubleshooting with the Basic Principles 137

Dedicated to the memory of my uncles:

*Rubert Southern,
who first took me to a golf course
when I was very young,*

and

*Ollie Scott,
who gave me my first set of clubs.*

Introduction:
Ruthlessness is Its Own Reward

According to my dictionary, *ruthless* means to be "without compassion; merciless."

I believe ruthlessness is the only logical approach to the game of golf. Golf is not about having either the best or the prettiest swing; no, it's about *scoring*. And I call this book **Ruthless Putting** because it is merciless in its approach to the one part of the game at which everybody can excel, regardless of their age, sex, or strength level—namely, stroking that little ball into the hole once you reach the green.

No part of the game is as rife with superstition and useless tradition than putting; in fact, one of my test versions of this book was called **The Way of the Putter**. It was built around a fake ancient text called the *I Putt* (pronounced *ee put*) and supposedly written by a mystic named Ho Lout. At first I thought it would be an entertaining way to cover the material.

In the end, I decided it was needlessly "cute" and canned it all. We've already made putting more complicated than it needs to be; I saw no reason to add to the confusion. I rewrote this book three or four times, using three or four different concepts, and finally reduced its size nearly 50% from the original manuscript. I hope that so much rewriting has made the message clearer.

And what is that message? Simply this: *Putting just isn't that hard.* If the history of the game teaches us anything, it's that there is no single putting method that works better than any other. Rather, we each have to find the stroke that works best for us. It's the putter who ruthlessly pursues this goal who eventually gains the confidence to beat any opponent.

10 Ruthless Putting

Fortunately, there are basic principles that every putter should follow, principles that can be easily adapted to any stroke. You don't need expensive training aids—in fact, I can almost guarantee you have the "equipment" you need for these lessons just laying around the house. All you really need is a willingness to let go of what you think you know. Once you learn the principles, you can spend your practice time working on your long game; your putting stroke won't need much practice to keep it in shape.

Because I focus on principles and don't want you to just copy "positions," I haven't included any photographs. Rather, you'll find *diagrams* illustrating the important points. Trust me, those diagrams are sufficient to help you understand everything you need to know to make your stroke work.

Believe it or not, there isn't really anything new in this book, but I can promise you that it's never been presented this way before. I begin by comparing the teachings of three well-known teachers—Dave Pelz, Stan Utley, and Bobby Jones—and finding their common ground. This provides us with seven basic principles agreed upon by teachers with three distinctly different putting styles, as well as providing a historical perspective that's usually missing.

I then apply these principles to four basic ways of stroking the ball, strokes that have been used by various successful players at various times over the past century. Rather than making you change your existing stroke to conform to some unreachable ideal, I'll show you how to determine which of these strokes most closely matches yours and how to capitalize on its strengths. And you'll learn why you should choose one grip over another in order to maximize the effectiveness of your stroke.

Then I'll teach you how to stroke the ball using golf teaching methods that have been used for decades—you'll recognize the teachers, and maybe even the methods themselves—but I'm going to show you how to apply them specifically to putting.

A large section of the book deals with the yips. In my studies I was shocked that no one seems to understand what they are or what causes them, despite how common the problem is. I've had yips before and I beat them, so I'll give you the simple technique I used. Even better, I'll show you how to avoid ever getting them again. (And you won't believe how simple it is!)

Introduction

Finally, I'll give you a troubleshooting guide to help you quickly detect and remedy any problems that pop up in your improved swing.

On occasion you'll see brief passages from other books, included primarily to ensure that I haven't misrepresented the original speaker. (Some of the Bobby Jones quotes refer to the full swing, not specifically the putting stroke, but I believe he would have agreed with my use of them.) I usually abbreviate the sources when I refer to them. These are the abbreviations and the books to which they refer:

- AOP *The Art of Putting,* by Stan Utley
- PB *Dave Pelz's Putting Bible,* by Dave Pelz
- BJOG *Bobby Jones on Golf,* by Bobby Jones
- PM *Putting Out of Your Mind,* by Dr. Bob Rotella

I also used Dr. Joe Parent's book **Zen Putting** as a reference, but there are no direct quotes from his book. References to other teachers often come from appearances they made on the Golf Channel (Dave Stockton immediately comes to mind), so I can't give you specifics beyond that; if I used a specific book or video, its name is mentioned.

And finally, there are a few things you should know to help you get the most from this book.

When you write about an activity like putting, which is practiced by a widely diverse group of people, the actual writing becomes more complicated than it should be. As a result, I have made some concessions in the name of simplicity. I'm not totally happy with these decisions, but they seemed to be the best way to eliminate potential confusion.

Two such decisions concerned the terms "putter" and "grip." A putter can be either a club or the player using the club. My guiding principle was to use whichever was clearer in the passage's context; but generally, I have used "putter" to refer to the person.

Likewise, the grip can refer to either the cushioned cylinder at the end of the putter shaft, or to the hand position with which that cylinder is held. I have chosen to refer to the hand position as a grip, and to call the cylinder a "handle."

Two other issues posed a greater problem. One of the beauties of putting is that neither sex has an advantage over the other, and the material in this book applies equally to both men and women. Unfortunately, the English language is sadly deficient when it comes to pronouns that refer to both sexes at once. While plural pronouns like *we*, *they*, and *theirs* aren't a problem, pronouns referring to an individual golfer who could be either male or female are another matter altogether. Since arbitrarily switching between *he* and *she*, *his* and *hers*, and *him* and *her* seems unnecessarily contrived to me, and since I refuse to use ridiculous contractions like *s/he*, *s/his*, and *s/him*, I've chosen to use masculine singular pronouns throughout. I think they are easier to read than the alternatives, and I hope no woman takes offense at my choice.

The other problem concerns all you lefthanders out there. The material here applies equally to you but, after experimenting with various other ways of referring to the two sides of the body, as well as doing two versions of all the diagrams, I finally decided the simple route was the clearest. Therefore, I have consistently approached the material as a righthander; lefthanders will merely need to substitute *left* for *right* and vice versa, and can simply "mirror" the diagrams. As with my female readers, I apologize for this inconvenience.

Unfortunately, both women and lefthanders are probably used to this situation, and I hope you'll both forgive me for taking the easy way out. I also hope you take great pleasure in using what you learn here against your less-than-sympathetic opponents!

Well, I think that pretty much covers all the bases. Now let's get to work and turn you all into truly ruthless putters!

Mike Southern
June 2009

RUTHLESS PUTTING

1 The Mind of the Ruthless Putter

There is the ball; there is the hole; there is the union of the two.

This union is the goal of the ruthless putter. He refuses to be satisfied with a technically perfect stroke, a mechanically simple stroke, or even an aesthetically pleasing stroke. He believes the union of ball and hole is the measure of a good putt, and the ability to achieve this union at will is the measure of a good putter.

The ruthless putter is not sidetracked by the peripheral issues that dominate most teaching. If the use of a certain technique gets the ball into the hole at will, he calls it a good technique. Or, to put it more poetically: For the ruthless putter, beauty is in the score of the beholder.

Do others laugh at his technique? The ruthless putter will heartily agree and even laugh along with them. After all, if the pigeons don't enjoy the game, they won't return for a second plucking.

Having said that, I must add that no putter, regardless of how good he is, makes every putt.

There are so many variables in the game, so many little things beyond our control that no reasonable person should ever expect otherwise. We have always missed many, perhaps most of our putts... and we always will, no matter what putting method we follow or what individual technique we may incorporate into our stroke. That's the nature of playing a game of skill in the real world, where wind and weather freely influence the behavior of the ball *after* it leaves the clubface.

Modern teaching rarely begins with the mental game; it may mention pre-shot routines and the like, but

Ruthless Putting

only after the player has had some degree of success learning other techniques. I don't think we can wait that long; far too many players believe that their putting ability (or playing ability in general) is a reflection of their value as a person. We don't need to look far to see a classic example of this.

When Kenny Perry didn't win at the 2009 Masters, he remarked that "great players" close the deal when they get the chance. Excuse me, but didn't Arnold Palmer, Seve Ballesteros, and Greg Norman all lose huge leads at majors? Does anybody question their greatness? And, I would like to point out that all of them blew those huge leads *after* they had been in contention and won majors. Kenny had only been in contention twice, and those tournaments were 13 years apart.

It was a remark made in the wake of disappointment, which was understandable; but I heard commentators agree with him, which was not. If I were a sports psychologist, I would have been greatly disappointed; apparently nobody is listening.

But here is where the mind of the ruthless putter separates him from the wannabes and makes him so dangerous: *He is mentally tough enough to judge his progress by his success and not by his inevitable failures.* Until we shed this ridiculous notion that our putting ability says something about what kind of person we are, we will find that putting well is only a dream… and no technique will change that.

Along similar lines, how often have you seen Tiger Woods make yet another miraculous putt, followed by this comment from an announcer: "He just seems to will them into the cup, doesn't he?" Do they really believe Tiger has some psychic power over the ball? I can't answer that question… but I'm certain that many of the people watching Tiger on TV believe that he does. (For that matter, I think many of the professionals Tiger plays against believe it.) A similar debate surrounded Jack Nicklaus at the height of his game.

The ruthless putter knows better. There is no magic in putting, no mystic force that gives one putter an advantage over another.

Neither does *ritual* benefit a putter. This superstition has found its way into our modern game through our practice sessions before the game, as well as through the putting routines we carry with us onto the course.

17 The Mind of the Ruthless Putter

A constant battle is waged in the modern game, over both putting and the game of golf as a whole. It's been characterized at times as a battle of mechanics against wizards, a struggle between the putter whose stroke appears overly mechanical and the putter who focuses on "feel." Which one is superior? More specifically, which putter holes the most putts?

To this end, golfers in general and putters in particular have developed an almost fanatical attachment to the use of pre-shot routines, believing that they will make it possible to play more consistently.

In a darker vein, we've come to believe that the lack of such a routine—or, heaven forbid, the actual *breaking* of an existing routine!—will cause our game to fall apart.

In some cases they do seem to help, but is this fixation on routines healthy? The putting routine has become surrounded by superstition and mysticism; unless we debunk the magic before we start, mastery of the putter will remain little more than a fantasy.

Bobby Jones once said that anybody attempting to turn putting into a science was doomed to disappointment; his routine appears to have been little more than bouncing the club once in front of and once behind the ball before stroking, and he appears to have preferred making the routine as short as possible. Dave Pelz has attempted to scientifically quantify every aspect of the swing—I readily admit that I have been enriched by his efforts—and he offers a great many variations for swing routines, stressing that the most important aspect is that the routine does not vary in the amount of time it takes. But no matter how much we study and dissect the subject, no matter what we try, consistency in putting continues to elude us. Just watch Pelz's star student, Phil Mickelson; although I consider him one of the masters of putting, his stroke—like Tiger's—turns from gold one day to lead the next. Putting, like all arts, will always defy our ability to quantify it.

And where science fails, folklore abounds. Putting routines have become the modern rabbit's foot, and sports psychologists our shamans. I don't have anything against sports psychologists, but do you really need a doctor to tell you that you're taking the game too seriously? That you've forgotten it's only a game, and that whether you win or lose tells people nothing

18. Ruthless Putting

about your value as a person? For such players, the routine becomes more magic than substance, and their psychologists often sanction such superstition under the guise of "entering a comfort zone."

This is little more than ritual and magic. Even the best players have bad days, and no amount of posturing can entice the gods to guide your ball into the cup; realize this, and then a putting routine can become a formidable ally in the game.

So... what should you expect from a putting routine? What is its purpose, and how does it accomplish its task?

Listen closely: *The purpose of the putting routine is simply to give you confidence by insuring that you have all the information necessary to make a good putt.* That's all.

Far too many putters treat their routine as a magic talisman that allows putting to become a subconscious act, an out-of-body experience where they are more observer than participant. They think that if they just repeat the routine over and over, never deviating from it in the slightest measure, they will develop an almost superhuman ability to get the ball in the hole. Pull the trigger, hole the putt.

When such techniques are used, it's no surprise that our putting becomes erratic.

The ruthless putter places more confidence in the mind than the technique. He values *intelligence;* to make putts, he must understand both the factors that influence the ball and the way he can best make use of them. But he also needs *determination;* sometimes success evades him, and only by continued application of intelligence can he reach his goal.

Ironic, isn't it? The ruthless putter refuses to place his trust in either mechanics or feel. He places his trust in his *mind.* The way of the ruthless putter is a journey toward better understanding.

A good putting routine engages the mind. It allows you to step up to your putt, confident that you are prepared to make a good stroke. And how does it accomplish this wonderful task? By making sure you have all the information necessary for the execution of a good stroke. To put it another way, a good putting routine allows you to know, beyond doubt, that you can stroke your putt on a good line and with a speed that gives it a reasonable chance to go in the hole.

And if you "complete your routine" but don't have that confidence... *you don't stroke the putt.* Putting

The Mind of the Ruthless Putter

routines are not sacred rituals, and the golf gods will not strike you down for violating them. If you aren't ready to putt, then you continue to gather information until you are. (Within reason, of course. This isn't brain surgery, so it shouldn't take ten minutes to get your line and speed.)

And, needless to say, if your routine repeatedly fails you, then you create a new routine. You control the routine, not the other way around.

A routine is basically a visualization. That word may conjure the idea of pictures—seeing a line drawn out on the green, or maybe seeing the ball rolling toward the hole. But the feel of how much effort to put into the stroke is also visualization. So is the feel of how the green slopes under your feet, and your judgment of how wind and grain will affect your putt. Aromas, tastes, and

The purpose of the putting routine is simply to give you confidence by insuring that you have all the information necessary to make a good putt. **That's all.**

sounds also affect our assessments. (It's true. How many times have you taken a deep breath on an especially fragrant course and just *knew* you were going to make that long curling putt?) Visualization involves all the senses; that's part of its mystique.

As you work your way through this book you'll gradually build a putting routine based on your own manner of preparation. You'll find many little tricks for helping you develop feel and rhythm and, by extension, confidence. Feel free to make these part of your routine as well, but realize there is no rule that mandates what to do before putting. Just ready yourself, then putt.

There is no magic to putting routines, just as there is no magic to mastering your putter. There is only the one great truth: *There is the ball; there is the hole; there is the union of the two.*

For the ruthless putter, the game on the green really is that simple... and he refuses to make it any harder than that.

2 The Basic Principles of Good Putting

With our minds hopefully cleared of unrealistic expectations, we can move on to our primary concern, the union of ball and hole.

Stripped of all the extraneous pretenses, this simple concept of "the union" reminds us that there are no pictures on the scorecard, no grades for how pretty or ugly our stroke is, and no extra credit for having the most mechanically perfect stroke.

In the end, all that matters is getting the ball into the cup.

But what's the best way to go about it? If the history of the game, with its wild variety of great putters, has taught us anything, it's that there is no single prescribed method for getting the ball into the hole. How can we possibly determine the most successful method?

Perhaps there is no single method, but there are principles to guide us in our pursuit. In this chapter I'm going to try and uncover those basic principles, primarily using the work of three outstanding teachers of the game—Dave Pelz, Stan Utley, and Bobby Jones. These great putters give us an overview not only of the best modern techniques, but a historical perspective as well. All have uniquely different ways of striking the ball as well, so any techniques they have in common are probably general principles that all putters can use, regardless of their chosen style.

This approach isn't the easiest, however. A casual reading of their teachings can lead one to assume that there is *no* agreement between them, and that you must choose to follow only one or end up hopelessly confused.

The Basic Principles of Good Putting

Don't be fooled by these apparent disagreements. Many of them are illusions brought on by their use of the same terms to mean different things, or of different terms being used to describe the same principle. In fact, I have uncovered no less than SEVEN putting principles on which all three agree. I believe these can serve as the basis of a solid putting game, no matter how you like to putt.

Don't be surprised if you recognize some or all of these principles. They are, after all, as old as the game itself.

(1) The clubface should remain square to the stroke path; the forearms should NOT rotate during the execution of the stroke.

While virtually every teacher in the game today agrees with this principle, most never state it so plainly. (Jones was an exception here.) Because this particular principle is so important to our study, I will go into some detail about how Pelz and Utley describe it in their respective methods. Let it serve as a glaring example of why there is so much confusion among us today.

Pelz says you should keep your clubface square to the *aimline* (that's the line on which you want the ball to start), while Utley says you should keep your clubface square to its *arc* (the line on which your clubhead travels as you make your stroke). Each accuses the other of manipulating the clubface: Pelz says the Utley method swings the clubhead from open to closed (that means the toe of the club swings past the heel), while Utley says the Pelz method manipulates the clubface from closed to open (the heel swings past the toe).

In fact, *neither* is manipulating the clubface at all.

Please note that I am using the term *path* to describe the movement of the clubhead as it swings back and forth during a stroke. The apparent conflict between the two is in the different clubhead path each uses.

Because the Pelz system considers both the 'aimline' and 'path' to be straight lines, keeping your clubface square to the aimline *is the same thing* as keeping your clubface square to the path. The Pelz method stresses a straight line path, so he tends to use 'aimline' most of the time. And because the Utley approach automatically assumes that every swing path is an 'arc' (curve), his aimline (which must be straight) can never be the same as his arc.

Ruthless Putting

The irony is that both are saying the exact same thing—namely, that *the clubface must remain square to the swing path*. But neither ever acknowledges the other teacher's differing terms and definitions—Pelz says paths are straight, while Utley says they're curved—even though they're talking about the same thing!

You can also see why each claims the other manipulates the club. Compared to a straight path, Utley does appear to open the clubface on the way back and close it as he strikes the ball; and compared to a curved path, Pelz appears to swing the heel of his club past the toe on the backswing, before opening it on the downswing. Each is 'correct,' and yet each is so wrong! Such things create havoc with any attempt to compare their different stroke philosophies.

As for not rotating the forearms... Stan Utley, after saying that the clubface "moves in a way that's square to the arc" (AOP 40), then says the clubface opens and closes due in part to a slight forearm rotation (AOP 107). *But it's physiologically impossible* to keep the clubface square to the stroke arc if you roll your forearms! So either Utley rolls his forearms or he keeps the clubface square, *but he can't do both*.

I'm going to spend an entire chapter dealing with forearm motion, both because it can be so confusing and because the motion is so essential to the other principles. For now, let me just say that Stan Utley may *feel* as if his forearms rotate, but they don't; the photos in his book prove that.

Incorporating this one principle into your stroke can rapidly improve your putting ability, so remember it!

(2) The putter should be held in a "parallel" grip, where both palms are parallel to the face of the putter and the back of the left hand faces the target.

That's pretty simple, isn't it? To put it a bit differently, the palm of your right hand faces the target. Think of pushing the ball toward the hole with your palm, and you can't help but get your hands in the right position.

(3) The putter should be held lightly, without tension in the arms or shoulders or hands.

Sam Snead, a fine teacher as well as a great player, used to say you should hold all your clubs as if you were holding a baby bird. And the writers of the movie *Bobby*

The Basic Principles of Good Putting

Jones: Stroke of Genius had Harry Vardon giving a young Bobby Jones the same advice, using the same image. Just as in the full stroke, you want to hold the putter no tighter than necessary, just tightly enough that you won't drop it when you swing it.

(4) The putter handle should be held so that the shaft aligns with the forearms.

You may have heard this principle stated in a slightly different way: *The putter handle should be held along the lifelines of the palms, so that the shaft aligns with the forearms.* Generally this is true, although Bobby Jones says in his putting film that he held the club lightly in his fingers. However, you can clearly see that the shaft of his putter, the notorious Calamity Jane, is still in line with his forearms. We'll look at his putting style later because I suspect many frustrated putters are using it, albeit incorrectly. For almost everyone else, the putter handle *will* rest in the lifelines of your palm when you align the shaft with your forearms.

(5) The putter should never follow an outside-to-inside path (a cut stroke).

You might not see the logic of this principle at first, but think about the club's movement during the stroke.

If you swing "around your body" as Utley recommends, there will be a zone of several inches where the clubhead is moving pretty straight toward the hole.

If you swing "straight back" as Pelz recommends, the clubhead is always moving toward the hole.

However, if you pull the club across the line as a cut stroke requires, the clubhead is always moving at an angle to the hole. If the clubface never moves straight toward the hole, then *the ball* will never move straight toward the hole.

Yes, that's a problem. The good news here is that fixing a cut stroke doesn't require a major retooling of your swing, and it's a pretty simple adjustment.

(6) The clubhead should travel on a long low path, as close to the ground as possible, both going back and through.

Other than the drive, where the ball is elevated on a tee, the putt is the only stroke that follows this rule. Save that downward chop for chip shots. But if you're hitting down now... again, don't worry. It won't require

Ruthless Putting

a complete swing rebuild to flatten your stroke; you'll be getting a good roll in no time at all.

(7) The lower body should not be rigid, neither should it be consciously moved. It should move no more than the natural execution of the stroke requires.

Another simple principle. Longer putts require a little body movement, while tap-ins need none at all. This one is largely a matter of relaxing, since way too many putters turn into statues over the ball. Perhaps that's why we call them "pigeons"...

That's a quick look at the Seven Basic Principles of Good Putting. We'll be spending the remainder of this book making them part of our putting stroke, regardless of what that stroke looks like now.

You can probably see that the principles divide naturally themselves into related groups.

- *Principles 1-4 make up a group that focuses on how the club is held.*
- *Principles 5-6 make up a group that focuses on how the club is swung.*
- *Principle 7 focuses on how we address the ball.*

We might also view these principles in terms of grip, tempo, and stance.

We'll discuss these principles in more detail as we move through the book. The most important thing to realize at this point is that *any* stroke using these principles can be a winner. You're on the verge of major improvement right now, no matter how strange your current putting stroke may look!

3 The Universal Move

Of all the basic principles, the first one is the most crucial because it has the most effect on the position of the clubface:

The clubface should remain square to the stroke path; the forearms should NOT rotate during the execution of the stroke.

Avoiding forearm rotation during the stroke is the primary mechanical skill necessary to putting success. This move, sometimes described as "keeping the clubface square to the path on which you stroke the ball," is generally treated as a difficult maneuver, one which requires much practice to master.

Nothing could be further from the truth! This is a skill we use every day; life would be very inconvenient if this movement were as difficult as most people believe. We need only transfer this skill to putting, and we can learn to do so quickly and easily.

All it takes is a simple drinking glass.

Try It with One Arm

Take the glass in one hand—either hand—and hold it so the open end is straight up. Don't pretend it's a putter or anything, just hold it the way you would if it was full of water and you were going to take a drink. Now move your forearm and hand to the side, as though you intended to set this glassful of water on a table.

I suppose there's a decent chance your forearm will rotate, and whatever was in the glass would pour out on the floor; but I'd be willing to bet that your forearm

Ruthless Putting

doesn't rotate at all. Your mind routinely guides your hand and arm this way; otherwise we would spend our days cleaning up the mess. You probably kept the glass upright *even though it was completely empty.*

Rotating your forearm is a natural move because of the way the arm joints and muscles move, but keeping the glass upright (which means your forearm didn't rotate at all) is also a perfectly natural move because you don't want to spill its contents. What causes us to choose one over the other?

It's the concept you hold in your mind, the way your mind perceives the move. Unless you're paying attention, you may not even be aware which concept is in charge until you see the results. Your mind simply thinks *Move your arm* and the natural motions of your body take over, possibly rotating the forearm and tilting the glass to the side. However, your mind might also think *The glass is full* and counteract that movement in order to keep the glass upright. The first thought was just a motion—*move your arm*—and the second was a purposeful motion—*keep the glass upright.*

This isn't a new concept for most of you. This is yet another example of *visualization,* but you probably never considered it in such simple terms.

The truth is, we visualize all the time... but we don't always do it *consciously.* Although it didn't matter this time, you can probably remember a time when you made this precise move with a full glass and shocked both yourself and your friends by spilling a drink all over them. And after you apologized, what did you say? "I wasn't thinking." What you meant was that your mind didn't visualize a forearm move with a full glass and, as a result, you didn't keep the glass upright.

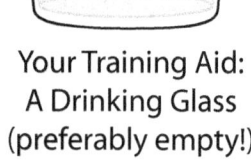

Your Training Aid:
A Drinking Glass
(preferably empty!)

Repeat this movement several times, paying attention to the difference in the way these two similar but conceptually different moves feel. They really are quite different, although neither seems to take more effort than the other; the effort is just focused in a different place. You may feel tension along the top of the forearm in the first case, along the bottom in the second. (You've probably never thought of it that way either, have you?

The Universal Move 27

Pay attention while you try the two moves; you really can feel that difference.)

I hope I've shown you that this forearm move is a very natural thing. But—and this is a big but—we used only *one* arm and hand in this test. What happens when we use *both* arms and hands?

Now with Both Arms

Let's try it again; this time, hold the glass with both hands. Hold the glass just tightly enough to avoid dropping it, move it from side-to-side. Did the glass tip over this time? And did it require any special effort to keep the glass upright?

I doubt it, because this is the natural way to move when you hold something with *both* hands. *Rotating the forearms when holding the glass in both hands is something you have to consciously decide to do.* If you had any tendency to tilt the glass at all, you probably tilted it forward, away from you—the only wrist movement possible without using the forearms.

What I find so interesting about this experiment is that, for most people, the position of their hands relative to their body doesn't seem to matter. You may have held the glass near waist level, or you may have held it near shoulder level; you may have made a fairly big shoulder turn without changing your arm position; you may have kept both elbows straight; you may have bent both elbows equally; or you may have allowed one elbow to bend downward as the other straightened so you could move the glass further to the side. But however you did it, the glass probably didn't turn over and "spill."

And it took no special effort to keep it that way, no matter how you chose to do it.

This is, as I said, a natural move. Try making the move in several of the positions mentioned above; can you identify what feels different about each one? Take note of these differences, because your putting stroke probably matches one of these moves with the glass rather closely.

You're probably getting bored, but there's one last glass experiment I'd like you to try.

Take your putting position and let the glass tilt forward until its "contents" pour out on the ground in front of you. Make your putting stroke and take special notice of your thumbs. Even though you're making the same movements that you just made, it *looks* really

Ruthless Putting

different, doesn't it? (You should be able to tell now whether your forearms are rotating or not. If not, lift your arms to shoulder-height and begin your putting swing there, letting your arms swing slowly from side-to-side as you lower them to your normal putting position.).

For the vast majority of you, your stroke will make an arc and your thumbs will always be "on top" of the glass, pointing directly away from you. Make a note of this feel; it means "no forearm rotation."

If you see any other result, keep working with the glass. Pay special attention to how it feels. Using the glass this way gives you an easy way to practice the proper move; just "pour the water out of the glass along the path of the putting stroke." It may feel as if you're pointing at the line of the putt with both of your thumbs. (Again, they should remain "on top" of the glass.) Or you might feel that the "butt end" of the glass always points toward your navel.

The important thing is to choose a visualization that works for you.

Using the glass this way will give you an easy image to draw on while you're out on the course.

All Squared Away

Now take a putter and grip it with a parallel grip... Ok, we haven't talked about grips, and won't for several chapters yet. That may seem a bit backward to most of you; most teachers *begin* with the grip because they believe that, since the grip is your only contact with the club, it's the most important fundamental of the stroke.

While the grip is your only contact with the club, the grip is more organic than fundamental. By *organic* I mean that the grip is determined by your stroke; you grip the club in a manner that helps you make the best of your chosen stroke. Certain grips will work well only with certain strokes, while other grips have universal application. When our overriding concern is simply to sink the putt, it makes more sense to find the stroke that works best and then find a matching grip. Otherwise, we face the prospect of finding a grip we like but are unable to use effectively because it doesn't suit the type of stroke we use best.

For the time being, just grip the club in such a way that your palms face each other and the thumbs of both hands form a straight line down the top of the handle. Don't overlap any of your fingers; all ten fingers should

The Universal Move 29

contact the surface of the handle. This is sometimes called a ten-finger grip, or a baseball grip; since it's the grip we generally use when picking things up, it should feel very natural to you, even if it isn't your regular putting grip.

Don't worry if the thumbs aren't perfectly placed down the center of the putter handle. If the right thumb is off a little to the right side and the left thumb is a little to the left side, that's ok. They may even overlap each other a bit; that's ok too. Just make sure your grip isn't turned so both thumbs are on the left or on the right—that's a sure recipe for rotating forearms.

Now, as I was saying...grip the putter with a parallel grip and stand up straight, just the way you did when

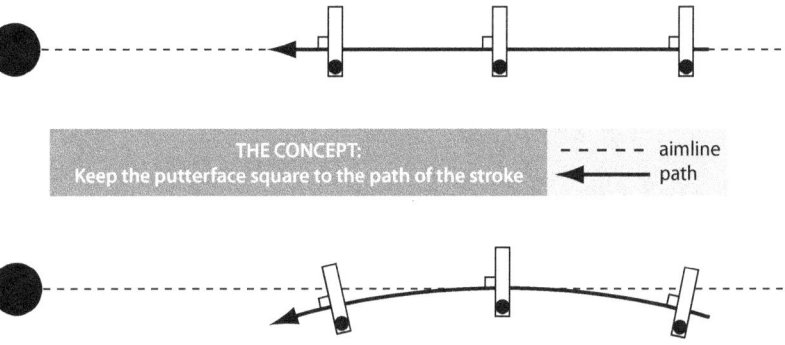

you held the glass. Cock your wrists so the shaft points straight up; this too should feel about the same as it did when you held the glass in both hands.

Swing the club from side-to-side, just as you did before with the glass. The weight of the putter head towering nearly three feet above your hands may make this a bit more difficult, but you don't have any real trouble keeping the shaft vertical, do you?

Now pretend there's a ball propped on a waist-high tee. Take your stance, lower your hands back to waist level, and tip your wrists forward so the shaft points away from you, parallel to the floor. This is almost your normal putting position. Repeat the side-to-side movement... AND WATCH THE TOE OF THE PUTTER. It should remain vertical, pointing skyward. It should not roll from side-to-side.

Ruthless Putting

And it should be a very simple task to accomplish.

Of course, this isn't an actual putting stroke; but if you took your normal stance, as you would to stroke a ball sitting at your feet, the stroke would feel almost exactly the same. If you create a flat vertical plane *a la* Dave Pelz, you should see the clubface remaining square; and if you stand taller throughout the stroke and make a "curved" stroke, the face of the putter will appear to open on the backswing, then 'square up' and close on the downswing. That's because we look down vertically through an inclined plane as the clubhead travels on an arced path.

So if you set up to make your normal stroke and want to see if your forearms are rotating or not, all you have to do is cock your wrists upward a little and make

> ## *The First Principle of Good Putting—that the forearms don't rotate during the swing—is the fundamental principle on which any stroke should be built.*

a practice stroke. If the toe of the putter continues to point straight up throughout the stroke, you know you're following Principle 1 perfectly.

And now you know what is perhaps the greatest secret of modern putting: Every year, weekend golfers spend hundreds of thousands, maybe millions of dollars on putting aids intended to help them make a stroke that is *perfectly natural*.

All you really need is a drinking glass and a little visualization practice.

If there is one thing I want you to take from this chapter, it's the knowledge that there is no bad putting stroke. As long as you follow the First Principle of Good Putting, you can move that ball into the hole with any stroke you feel comfortable using. **This is the big secret that all good putters know; it's why they succeed when so many others fail.**

Let me prove it to you...

Stroking the Ball

Drop a ball on the floor and pick a target to serve as your 'hole'. Then take your putter and step up to address

The Universal Move

the putt. We aren't worried about the actual method of stroking the ball at this point; we just want to set up and move the putter in a way consistent with Principle 1.

Aim at your target and grip your putter the way we did earlier and hit the ball.

That's the sum total of your instructions.

I don't care how far apart your feet are. I don't care whether you set up square, open, or closed. I don't care whether your weight is more on your left foot or your right foot. I don't care how many practice strokes you take. I don't even care where the ball is in your stance. Although, if I might make a suggestion...

A good rule of thumb is simply to set up with your hands over or slightly ahead of the ball. This will cause the shaft to lean slightly forward at setup, which may feel a bit odd to many of you, but it's an easy way to place the ball in a consistent position. If you let your arms hang straight down at setup, then position yourself so the ball is under your hands, you assure that the ball is always in the same position *relative to your hands and stroke*.

With this technique, ball position is determined by the way you set up, rather than your setup being determined by the ball position. This is why I say it's more organic, and you'll probably see more consistency of contact.

Now, make a stroke and hit the ball. Just let your shoulders and arms move however feels good to you, take the club back and let it swing through. Your key thought here is simply *no forearm rotation*. Just stroke the ball and see where it goes; you might be pleasantly surprised at how well you stroke it. Make this stroke a few more times—remember, no forearm rotation—and see if your putting improves. Can you putt like this without tensing up?

The First Principle of Good Putting—that the forearms don't rotate during the swing—is the fundamental principle on which any stroke should be built.

Does this move change your stroke from the way you normally swing? If so, you have identified a problem with your original stroke, because following this putting principle will eliminate a lot of excess movement in the arms.

There are several effective ways to stroke the ball once your forearms start to behave. Let's look at some of them now.

4 Meet the Four Basic Strokes

With so many teachers and so many putting methods to choose from, I suppose the most common question putters ask is "Which stroke is the best stroke?" For example, Dave Pelz says his is the simplest, while Stan Utley says his is the most natural. Can they both be right?

Perhaps the better question is "Which stroke is the best stroke for *me*?" Everyone seems to think that the answer to their putting woes is (a) a new putter or (b) a new stroke. That's especially true after a pro adopts some bizarre new stroke, begins to putt better, and starts a fad.

Are there truly "right" and "wrong" ways to putt? Maybe, maybe not. But clearly some ways of putting are better than others. And this is further complicated by a paradox of sorts: Simple strokes aren't always natural, and natural strokes aren't always simple.

A simple stroke can be supremely unnatural; moving the putter straight back and through while maintaining a constant height above the ground is a simple concept, but such a move can be extremely unnatural for some people to perform.

Likewise, a natural stroke isn't always simple: the classic example is a stroke where the forearms rotate during the stroke. Such a movement may feel very natural and can performed with little difficulty, but the movement of the clubhead during that stroke is so complex that consistency is nearly impossible.

What we need is a stroke that is both simple *and* natural—a stroke which is easy to repeat and simple to use. I call this a *low-maintenance* stroke, because such

Meet the Four Basic Strokes

33

a stroke should be able to produce repeatable results with very little practice.

But is this the mindset of the typical golfer? Hardly. He generally learns a new stroke because he imagines he has identified some problem in his current one—poor aim, for instance—and then he attempts to fix this single aspect of the game. But of course, putting is not just about poor aim. In the end, not only has he ignored the other equally important elements of his swing, but his obsession has insured a flawed stroke with which he will never be satisfied.

The ruthless putter, on the other hand, seeks a low-maintenance stroke. In finding a stroke that is both

> *The ruthless putter seeks a low-maintenance stroke. In finding a stroke that is both simple and natural, he assures that he will improve in all areas of his putting.*

simple and natural, he assures that he will improve in all areas of his putting.

I have categorized these strokes into four general styles. Most effective putters will use some variation (or combination) of these moves.

Why four? Why not three, or five, or forty-two? For that question I have no answer. Of one thing I'm certain—there must be more than one stroke because we all have slightly different bodies. A five-foot-tall man won't use the same stroke as a six-footer; a man of "ample girth" will not stroke the ball the way a slim woman does. Perhaps it's a simple matter of tall, short, thick, and thin… or perhaps tall, short, flexible, and inflexible.

In any case, these four strokes are our best choices.

The Four Styles

All the following information will be repeated as I cover each stroke, but I want you to have a clear overview of how they differ from each other.

Basically, I've characterized all four putting styles both by a motion and by the part of the body where each is primarily felt:

Ruthless Putting

- the shrug stroke, felt in the neck muscles
- the hug stroke, felt in the back muscles
- the fold stroke, felt in the elbows
- the pop stroke, felt in the hands

Just to get you oriented, these strokes relate to our three teachers like this:

- *The shrug stroke is similar to the Pelz stroke.*
- *The hug stroke is similar to the Utley stroke.*
- *The fold stroke is the one I think people use most, although it's not talked about much. Among the pros, Jack Nicklaus used a variation of the fold, and I would also include the "claw" in this group.*
- *And the pop stroke is how Jones putted… but most people would never recognize it as such since an authentic pop stroke is very different from what most people expect.*

The strokes can also be differentiated by whether the arms work as a unit or not.

In the first two strokes, the arms work together to maintain an unchanging triangle throughout the stroke:

- *Shruggers form a triangle with the hands and both shoulder joints.*
- *Huggers form a triangle with the hands and both elbow joints.*

In the second two, the arms move independently during the stroke:

- *Folders usually keep the left arm straight and bend the elbow of the right arm to power the stroke. In addition, their shoulders don't move much except at the extremes of the stroke.*
- *Poppers usually keep the right arm slightly bent and use the left arm to power the stroke. The right wrist is used only as a hinge, not a power source.*

Although we haven't talked about them yet, certain stroke styles tend to favor certain grips and stances as well, the claw being a good example. We'll discuss those preferences as we go.

Also, you should notice that not all of the gizmos you can order on TV will work with all strokes. Take those

Meet the Four Basic Strokes

braces that hold your forearms in a triangle throughout the swing, for example. They may help shruggers and huggers, but these devices will actually hinder improvement for folders and poppers.

Are there more ways to putt than these? Of course.

Are there more low-maintenance ways to putt than these? Perhaps, but I don't know what they are.

The key term here is *low-maintenance*. You need a stroke that doesn't take a lot of practice to use effectively. Almost all effective putting strokes that the weekend golfer cares about are variations of these four basic strokes.

Most importantly, all of these strokes can be made without rolling your forearms. Having learned this principle in the last chapter, you shouldn't have any trouble with the concept of a square clubface... but each of these strokes attains this position through a slight variation of the technique I taught you in the last chapter. We'll identify what style you're currently using in the next four chapters.

What Makes the Big Four So Low-Maintenance?

So now you know what the four low-maintenance strokes are and that, if your stroke doesn't match one of them exactly, you can use them as models to adjust your own stroke. You know that low-maintenance is the way to go because you can putt well without a lot of practice. And let's face it, it just makes sense.

So let's say you're sold. The question remains... just how do you do that?

What is it that makes these four strokes so low-maintenance?

Understand this: the Seven Principles describe the consensus about what makes a *good and usable* stroke, not necessarily a low-maintenance stroke. A stroke can take a lot of practice to maintain and still be good and usable; it's just that a weekend player doesn't have that kind of time. To my knowledge, nobody has ever tried to determine what a low-maintenance stroke is.

Until now. I can see three primary distinctions of such a stroke.

Obviously, a low-maintenance stroke follows the Seven Principles. Plenty of players use strokes that take no practice but don't make putts. The Seven Principles ensure that the stroke can sink putts. And since the gist of the Seven Principles is about keeping the clubface,

Ruthless Putting

forearms, and palms all square to the line of the putt, we'll call that our first trait of a low-maintenance stroke.

Second, a low-maintenance stroke doesn't use the wrists as a source of power. This isn't directly stated in the Seven Principles, but most teachers agree that this makes a stroke undependable... even with a lot of practice. Billy Casper, one of the greatest putters of the game, used to putt this way but said he changed because it was just too much work to keep it in shape.

Finally (and this is related to the second point), a low-maintenance stroke doesn't lock the forearms against the body. Forearm freedom is necessary both to prevent a stroke from becoming wrist-powered and to allow the use of a low-maintenance power source. I'll focus on that power source in the tempo chapter.

A Cautionary Tale: The Sad Case of Sam Snead

By the time you finish these next four chapters, you may feel that I've spent way too much time talking about the details and techniques of low-maintenance strokes in general and the Big Four in particular. If putting is the very simple affair I'm making it out to be, why belabor the point? If a low-maintenance stroke is basically just 1) a square relationship between the clubface, palms, and forearms, and 2) a low-maintenance source of power, why make all these lists of traits and principles?

I think the example of Sam Snead will explain my concerns best.

For those of you too young to remember him (I only remember his later years), Slammin' Sam Snead was one of the longest drivers in history. (If you can catch some of the *Celebrity Golf* show repeats on the Golf Channel, you can see Sam in his prime.) He won more than anybody on tour—82 wins here, 135 worldwide—and he's the oldest winner of a PGA Tour event in history at 52 years, 10 months. He was a fitness buff long before Tiger and maybe even Gary Player came along—he was weight-lifting without letting anybody know—and could kick the top of a seven-foot doorframe from a standstill well into his 70's.

But Sam's record could have been so much better if he hadn't fallen prey to the yips.

In his 1953 book **Natural Golf** he included a chapter called "Putting the Natural Way" where he described the changes he made to combat the yips. Unfortunately, those changes failed him sometime after the book

Meet the Four Basic Strokes

was published, and his struggles with the putter have become the stuff of legend.

Still, he left us enough info in that book to tell us how it happened. The main things we need to know are on pages 105 and 106.

Originally, Snead was (by his own description) a wrist putter who used a reverse-overlap grip and powered the stroke predominately with his right hand. This was a pretty common method of putting during his time but, as Billy Casper said, it's a recipe for disaster. Wrist putting is too undependable.

The changes he made sound promising. He changed his stance, resting his right forearm against the upper part of his right leg, and he made sure his hands didn't touch his body when he stroked the ball. Then he changed his power source from the right hand to both hands—in his own words, he "now stroke[s] the ball evenly with both hands and without the emphasis on the right hand that once characterized my stroke."

STOP RIGHT THERE. Although it sounds promising, you should now know that Sam is doomed to fail. Why?

As you'll see later, this pop stroke he designed is flawed. So what if Sam's hands don't touch his body? By anchoring his forearm, Sam eliminates the forearm movement a dependable low-maintenance swing requires. For all the changes, Sam Snead is *still* a wrist putter. He's powering the stroke with two hands now instead of one, and he's stooped over more, but that's about it.

He hasn't changed one thing that matters!

That's why I'm going to spend so much time on these strokes and how they are properly performed. It's easy to make what appear to be drastic changes without helping your game, but it's also easy to make minor changes that cause rapid and sustainable improvement... as long as you know what you're doing.

Take as much time as you need to study the next four chapters. In it are the keys to making your stroke function as well as those of the great putters in golf history. Combine the Seven Principles with a working knowledge of these four putting styles, and you can eliminate virtually any problem plaguing your game.

Pick a stroke, any stroke...

So you may be wondering... which of these strokes do I recommend? Which is the best?

Ruthless Putting

The answer is... I recommend them *all*. The best stroke... well, that depends on you.

Every teacher says his or her stroke is the best, and that shouldn't surprise you. Why would they waste time teaching a stroke they didn't believe in? Life is too short for that. And most teachers base their recommendations on work with pros—at least, the best-known teachers do. Let's face it, if you're a well-known teacher, it's because you have well-known students... and that generally means professionals. (Charles Barkley is another matter altogether.)

But since this is a book for weekend golfers, let me repeat myself yet again: Pros have hours to practice, *you don't*. And no matter what they say, a great short game won't lower your score until you can get the ball within scoring range in two strokes. (I know this to be true because I've been there; I had a killer short game but still struggled to break 100.) If you're in this boat, you don't need to waste your practice time *putting*. Putting is easy; if you know and apply the Seven Principles, you can hole putts with almost any stroke. Then you can devote your practice time to the rest of your game.

In fact, by the time you finish the next few chapters, you'll probably know more about your own putting mechanics than many experienced professionals know about theirs. The names I've given these strokes, while a bit off-the-wall, are highly descriptive; they will give you vivid pictures of the distinctive moves that make each stroke work. They're based on the *feel* of the strokes, and you'll find that these are very common feelings indeed.

In addition, I suspect you'll discover that no matter how unusual you may think your stroke is, you're still probably using a hug, shrug, fold, or pop stroke. (Or some combination—pick two, any two.) All are perfectly good strokes. If you're having problems, you're probably violating one of the Seven Principles. And if you start following the Principles more closely, your putting will improve dramatically.

Yes, it's as simple as that.

By the time we're done, you'll know that the best stroke for you is... YOUR STROKE.

5 The Shrug Stroke

The shrug is the basic Dave Pelz style. Some teachers feel this isn't a natural move, but I disagree. This is a common move for many people, one that they do without even thinking much about it.

Remember: Shruggers form a triangle with the hands and both shoulder joints, and that triangle remains constant throughout the stroke.

You feel the shrug mainly in your neck, and what distinguishes this stroke from the others is its attempt to keep the putting stroke in a vertical rather than an inclined plane. The method for doing this can be described with several different terms; "rocking the shoulders" is a common one. I liken it to a shrugging motion because I think most people can relate to that.

We'll build the basic shrug move step-by-step. You haven't put your drinking glass away yet, have you? It will help you avoid forearm rotation while learning the mechanics of all the basic strokes.

1) First, stand up straight and just shrug your shoulders. Let both shoulders move up, then let them both drop. Think about picking up two suitcases, then setting them down. That's a pretty natural move, isn't it?

2) Now try alternating the shoulders. Lift one up while lowering the other, then switch. Right side up, left side down; left side up, right side down... you get the idea. It's kind of a see-sawing motion.

3) Now let's put this into a swinging motion. If you've never tried this swing before, the easiest way to feel this properly is to take your putting stance... but set up so that your rear end is planted firmly against a

wall. It's easier to feel the proper motion of this swing if your bottom can't rotate when you first try it.

From this position (you may feel that you're propped against the wall) let both arms hang straight down and clasp your hands around that glass again, as if it were a putter. (Remember, you're "pouring" the contents out along the line of the putt.) Keep your arms straight; it may feel very stiff, but that's ok when you're just trying this for the first time. Just let your arms swing back and forth as if they were the pendulum of a clock. Think about lifting those suitcases one arm at a time, or see-sawing your shoulders—whichever is the clearest image for you.

The important thing is to keep both hips against that wall because this isn't a rotary motion. This is a *vertical* motion; as long as your hands are hanging on a straight

The Shrug Stroke

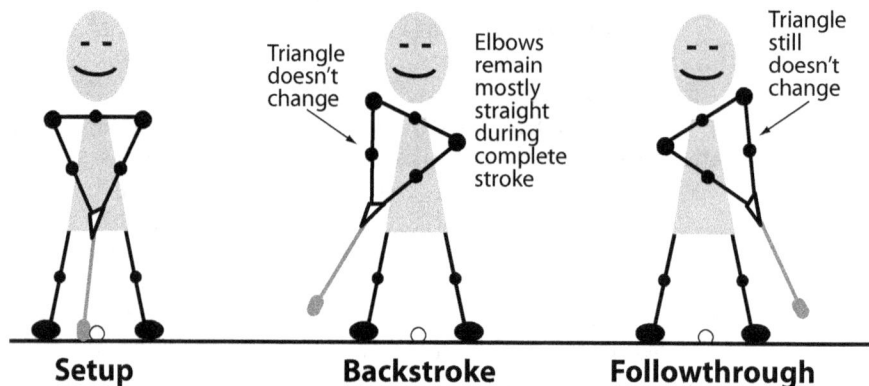

Setup   Backstroke   Followthrough

ball position shown for reference

line vertically beneath your shoulders, you should be able to swing the glass back and forth without rotating your forearms. (Don't stress over having your hands perfectly beneath your shoulders. Your forearms will maintain their position throughout the swing without much effort on your part if you shrug vertically.)

A hint: Rounding your shoulders may make this move easier. I know most teachers want you to stand more erect when you putt, with your hips stuck out a bit and your back straight, but that can make this style of putting harder than it needs to be.

Also note that, once you bend over into a putting stance, the angle at which you shrug changes. It's still

The Shrug Stroke

vertical; it's just that now "vertical" means that your shoulders move at an angle to your spine rather than parallel to your spine as it did when you stood straight up.

If you've ever picked up something heavy, you'll recognize this position right away. The difference is that you don't lift both shoulders at once.

4) When you feel comfortable enough with this move and can relax your arms a bit, try doing it with a putter. The clubhead won't be directly beneath your hands (more on that in a minute), but don't let that bother you. *It's the position of your hands and the vertical shrug of your shoulders* that keeps the forearms from rolling and the clubface square to the line of the stroke.

This is a good place to take a brief pause and see how the Seven Principles of Good Putting apply to the shrug.

One question that comes to mind is... can you still hold the putter shaft in line with your forearms? Principle 4 says we should try, but the arms hang *straight down* in the shrug and the USGA sets a maximum lie angle of 80°. (You'll find more about this when we talk about equipment.) To keep the shaft in line with your forearms, you'd have to hold the putter up on its toe, wouldn't you?

To avoid this problem, you'll have to bend your elbows slightly and move your hands a bit closer to your body. To get in that position, you'll have to bend over quite a bit, and back problems may prevent you from doing so. While theoretically anybody can shrug, *it clearly works best for tall people.* Dave Pelz and his star pupil, Phil Mickelson, are both well over six feet tall.

Although I'm easily a couple of inches short of the six-foot mark, I can shrug pretty well... but I had to build a special putter before I got really good at it. My putter is considerably shorter than normal, with a heavier head. (For those of you interested in such things, that putter is only 32 inches long and uses the head from a belly putter, which weighs around 400 grams—roughly twice that of a standard clubhead.)

Even with a longer putter, I would still have to bend over quite a bit. If you have back problems that make you uncomfortable doing so, then no matter how simple it is, the shrug stroke may not be the best stroke for you.

Along the same lines, if you can't bend over enough to allow a straight stroke back and through, you can end up with a cut stroke, which violates Principle 5. The shrug requires a solid consistent setup; again, if you have trouble doing this, the shrug might not be the stroke for you.

The other principle that may give you problems is Principle 7, concerning lower body movement. The need to stroke on a straight path means you need to be still, and this could cause you to tense up.

You may find it takes some stress off your efforts to keep your lower body still if you widen your stance. Pelz suggests a stance shoulder-width or wider, but this is a personal matter; if you can stay still with your feet only six inches apart, that's fine too.

You'll hear me say this over and over, so you might as well get used to it: If you want to make your stroke function at a high level of consistency with minimal practice, it's critical that you understand that *the goal is not to create an ideal stroke but to understand how your own stroke differs from the ideal, as defined by the Seven Principles of Good Putting*. This way, you can make only the alterations necessary to compensate for the way your stroke is different... and leave the rest untouched.

In other words... if it ain't broke, don't fix it. The more instinctive your movements are, the more consistent they will be.

For many of you, the strug stroke will seem like the Holy Grail. It isn't as unnatural as some people claim; many of you will find a vertical motion much easier to repeat with consistency than a rotary one.

Although I'm a bit shorter than the ideal for shrugging, I find the vertical motion feels pretty natural for putting. This movement is inherently less likely to cause forearm rotation than almost any other stroke. By the same token, a shrug stroke can be an endless source of grief if it gets off-line.

But don't be surprised if the shrug doesn't feel good to you, or if you simply can't do it. There is no perfect putting stroke. All strokes have plusses and minuses, and the wise putter finds the one that most closely suits him, then learns from it.

The shrug stroke isn't the only good way to putt. If it doesn't suit you, don't worry; one of the other strokes surely will.

6 The Hug Stroke

The hug is a variation of the stroke Stan Utley teaches. You might also think of it as the opposite of the shrug, although the two have a lot in common.

Remember: Huggers form a triangle with the hands and both elbow joints, and that triangle remains constant throughout the stroke.

Let's grab our trusty drinking glass again. Hold it with both arms out straight, the way you did for the shrug... but relax your arms, letting your elbows bend slightly as if pulling the glass toward you. (This reminds me of a hugging motion, hence the name.)

Now, standing up straight and maintaining that relaxed gap between your arms and body, swing the glass from side-to-side. You're moving your shoulders in a plane parallel to the floor and perpendicular to your spine. If you leaned forward into your putting stance, your shoulders would still rotate perpendicular to your spine. You shouldn't feel any upward motion, the way you did when you "shrugged"; this motion is much more rotary.

Congratulations. You have just performed the basic hug.

It's worth noting a couple of similarities between the hug and the shrug.

Like the shrug, the arms are not manipulated during the hug. We take our stance, extending our arms in a comfortable position, and we maintain that position throughout the stroke. While shruggers keep the arms mostly straight because they hang down, huggers stand more erect and maintain some elbow bend—sometimes quite a bit—throughout the stroke. This means the hugger often uses a longer shaft on his putter.

Ruthless Putting

As stated earlier, the movement of the shoulders during the hug feels more rotary versus the vertical feel of the shrug. Compared to the shrug, which mainly uses the trap muscles, the hug focuses on the lower back, side, and ab muscles. Perhaps because it uses the lat and trunk muscles more, the hug feels *bigger* to me.

You probably noticed that both the hug and the shrug are primarily upper body moves. The hug sometimes requires a wide stance for stability, but you can usually perform it from a very narrow stance without swaying. This is because of the hug's more upright stance. When Stan Utley says the lower body doesn't move much, he isn't telling you to hold your lower body still; your lower body simply doesn't move much unless the hug stroke is huge.

The Hug Stroke

Note: Elbows are slightly bent, not straight

Notice that the club has not traveled back as far as in the shrug stroke

Shoulders move back and around rather than up and down

Elbows remain slightly bent during complete stroke

Notice that the club has not traveled forward as far as in the shrug stroke

Setup   **Backstroke**   **Followthrough**

ball position shown for reference

You may find that the hug feels more natural than the shrug; but then again, you may not. Although the hug (as I had you perform it earlier in this chapter) feels natural to me, I think it feels less natural when done from a normal putting position. I don't think that either stroke *should* feel entirely natural; they may be based on natural moves, but they have been altered for the not-so-natural process of striking a ball while standing to the side. There is artifice here; "naturalness" is something of an illusion in a putting stroke.

Now, regarding the application of our Seven Principles to the hug...

Principle 1 (keep the forearms from rotating) can sometimes be a problem with the hug. Because the

The Hug Stroke

trunk muscles are more involved and the triangle formed by the hands and elbows is smaller, the elbows tend to bend slightly and the tension in your arm muscles changes as you turn; that can cause you to rotate your forearms. This needn't be a problem if you're aware of it, but it does tend to be a bigger problem for the hugger than for the shrugger.

The swing path of the hug can be a beautiful thing to behold... unless you start bending and unbending your elbows excessively. Then you can run afoul of Principle 6 (make a long low backswing) because the clubhead will change heights during the swing, which will cause inconsistent contact with the ball. Mis-hits affect both direction and distance, so you should be aware of this potential problem also.

Finally, although the hug is a fairly relaxed swing to make, especially in comparison with the shrug, you can still fall into the trap of stiffening your lower body (a violation of Principle 7).

One thing I view as an advantage of the hug (and which Dave Pelz would call a disadvantage) is the curved arc the clubhead follows during a stroke. If the shrug is off-line, it's *always* off-line and it can take a lot of work to straighten it out. But as long as a hug stroke is made in a consistent manner—that is, as long as the arc is repeatable—it's merely a matter of finding a spot on that arc where the clubface will send the ball straight toward the hole. (That's not as hard as it sounds. If you're pushing the ball, move it forward in the stance; if you're pulling the ball, move it back in the stance. It's pretty easy to find the best spot.)

I suppose you could argue that the hug is the most natural stroke just because we hug people more often than we carry luggage. But the hug can go as badly out-of-whack as any other stroke, so I'll withhold judgment on that.

Hmmm...

If the shrug and the hug are both pretty natural, why do the pros who use them seem to need so much practice?

I suspect there are two reasons.

The first lies in the *posture* of the putting stroke. While both the shrug and the hug are natural moves when we stand normally, neither feels totally natural when we take our stance over the ball. From that posture, the most natural move is a *blended* one—part shrug and part hug, part lifting and part turning. It makes sense, doesn't it? The shoulders must turn to maintain the unchanging triangles preferred by both strokes; but that turn also causes extra tension in our shoulders, so we tend to lift them slightly as we do so.

And when we say that the shrug and the hug are natural moves, we really should hedge a bit and say they're *based* on natural moves. They're close enough to make them easy to learn, but they still may require a little practice..

And the second reason? The shrug and the hug are basically *pure* moves, either all vertical (against gravity) or all horizontal (or at least rotating perpendicular to the spine). This means, for example, that both strokes are easier to do if you stand perfectly erect; but the act of putting doesn't allow that. I find it's nearly impossible to do a respectable shrug if I don't roll my upper back and shoulders forward a bit; and no matter how hard I try, the hug always feels like I'm reaching for the ball. Not everyone will feel the same, but it certainly affects my performance of the stroke.

It may influence yours as well.

How many of the natural, relaxed motions that you make on any given day are isolated movements using only one set of muscles? Not very many, are there? When we go about our daily chores, or play games, or just stretch... how many of these movements use our whole body? Almost all of them.

To me, the most amazing aspect of this is how little attention we pay to these movements, and yet we perform some very complex actions with an ease that boggles the mind. (At least, it boggles the mind struggling to organize fifteen swing thoughts during a drive.) We may not perform those actions perfectly, but we perform them acceptably... and there's a part of our mind that rebels against any attempt to carefully perform a pure movement, that simply says, "Be quiet and just *do it!*"

The practical result is that most putters use a stroke that is neither a straight back-and-forth motion nor a pronounced arc. Instead, we get a move that is *nearly* vertical, but that also moves *slightly* to the inside on the way back and *slightly* around us on the way through. This is an animal that most teachers are not prepared to tame, preferring instead to tout the virtues of a single pure move... whatever that move may be.

The Hug Stroke 47

Does this describe your situation? THEN DON'T LET IT BOTHER YOU. Purity of motion is a goal—perhaps even a worthy one—but the ruthless putter recognizes that *such a goal may not be worth the price*. All the frustration, all the practice time, all the expensive lessons and equipment... and for what purpose? To learn how to launch a tiny ball on a perfect line... which an imperfect green will redirect more times than not!

Believe it or not, golf is a forgiving game... at least on the greens. You don't have to hit your putts perfectly to sink your fair share. But obsessing over your stroke will certainly destroy your game.

I know I sound like a broken record, but if you follow the Seven Principles of Good Putting, you'll learn how to make your stroke work whether you have a "pure" stroke or not. Trust me on this one.

*When we say that the shrug and the hug are natural moves, we really should hedge a bit and say they're **based** on natural moves. They're close enough to make them easy to learn, but they still may require a little practice.*

Both the shrug and hug strokes have survived the test of time because they are sound strokes that work for many people... but **many** isn't the same as **all**. They may not be the best strokes for **you**.

Fortunately, there are other possibilities...

7 The Fold Stroke

In the first two strokes, both arms work together as a single unit. This is the technique preferred by most teachers these days, but it wasn't always so. In the past, the putting stroke was thought to be a small version of the full swing.

In this traditional view of the full swing, both arms work together but each performs a slightly different role. One arm primarily steadies and guides the club, while the other provides the primary power source.

Our two remaining strokes fit this view. I call the first of these a *fold* stroke, because the right elbow folds on the backswing. It reminds me somewhat of swinging a bat or an axe.

However you choose to describe it, most modern teachers would use the word "heretical."

Remember: Folders usually keep the left arm straight and bend the elbow of the right arm to power the stroke. In addition, their shoulders don't move much except at the extremes of the stroke.

First, let's get the basics of the fold stroke. Compared to any other stroke, they're extremely simple.

The easiest way to understand the fold stroke is to take the glass in both hands and extend your arms straight out in front of you at shoulder height. Hold the glass vertically, as if it was full of water.

Now, without "spilling" any, move the glass as far as you can to your right without turning your shoulders. When you finish, your right elbow will be bent nearly 90° and your left arm will still be nearly straight.

By anybody's definition, your left arm has *folded* over your chest. Of course, this is an extreme version of

The Fold Stroke

the fold stroke's main move; from a normal stance, the folding of the arm isn't nearly so noticeable.

The fold is probably the most commonly-used stroke because it's the only stroke that can be *blended* with all the other strokes. For example, in many cases the folder will add a little shoulder turn, making it appear more like a hug to the untrained eye. This can frustrate attempts at improvement, since the two strokes have different mechanics—mechanics that differ largely because folders normally don't turn the shoulders much at all. But a fold-hug blend can be a deadly combination, since its arc is much closer to a straight line stroke than a regular hug.

Likewise, some folders try to adopt the shrug's consistent arm-and-shoulder triangle. Such putters can become very frustrated if they believe they are shrugging; the shrug-fold blend *always* creates a shallow arc, not

The Fold Stroke

Setup — **Backstroke** (Shoulders don't move much; Elbow moves out; Elbow doesn't change) — **Followthrough** (Shoulders tilt just a little bit at contact; Elbow moves back into position)

ball position shown for reference

the straight line stroke of the true shrug. But this blend can also work well, because that arc gives it some of the benefits of the hug stroke.

The fold's simplicity makes it an instinctive choice for the new golfer who hasn't been taught another method. It's versatile; because it doesn't require a lot of body rotation, it can be used effectively by a wide variety of body types. And it's good for those with tender backs and other physical problems—it requires very little trunk rotation, and can be performed from a reasonably erect posture.

The reason for this is that *independent arm motion*. Both the shrug and the hug set the arms at the start of the stroke and move them as a unit, with each arm remaining in its original position.

Not so with the fold. One arm remains straight throughout the stroke; the other bends on the backstroke, then straightens on the forward stroke. (Occasionally you'll meet a folder who folds one arm on the backswing and the other on the followthrough, but this is the exception.)

A common misconception is that the fold causes a "wrist breakdown" after contact. Unless a player is pushing the club through impact rather than just letting it swing, that apparent breakdown is actually a gradual hinging movement that happens throughout the swing, not a sudden "give" at the end of the swing. Our bodies are built to function this way, so unless the swing is stopped abruptly as the club nears the ball, the clubface position is not altered and the clubhead won't be flipped upward at contact. Solid contact will be made and the ball will track along its intended line.

The wrists are certainly more involved in the fold stroke than in either of the other strokes we've discussed so far, but *the wrists do not provide power during the swing*. Let me repeat that, with emphasis: **THE WRISTS DO NOT PROVIDE POWER DURING THE SWING.** We'll discuss this more in the tempo chapter, but understanding this now is critical to proper execution of the fold stroke. The hinging of the wrists is controlled totally by the movement of the arms and club; you simply hold the club, and the natural mechanics of the stroke take care of the rest.

That wrist flex actually helps minimize forearm rotation by keeping the clubface square to the arc; and that arc is very shallow, almost flat, even with a very upright stance. That, along with the quiet body so characteristic of the shrug stroke, makes the fold very consistent.

There are, as usual, a couple of potential problem areas the fold stroke can have in relation to the Seven Principles:

If you start using the wrists to power the stroke, you can develop a cut stroke (a violation of Principle 5) or even a hook stroke. The bright side of this is that, because of the independent arm action, correcting this problem doesn't involve all the tinkering often required to fix a path problem with the hug or the shrug.

The Fold Stroke

Using the wrists can also get you in the habit of lifting the putter on the backswing, which will prevent the low takeaway recommended by Principle 6. This can also be caused by bending *both* elbows when you start the club back—a relatively simple problem to fix.

I really like the fold stroke. It's an extremely simple and consistent stroke to make, and it just *feels* good to most people. If you pay attention next time you see a child making his first attempts at putting, chances are good you'll see a fold stroke.

The Nicklaus Fold Stroke... and the Claw

Jack Nicklaus went his own way when it came to golf, whether it was an upright swing when Hogan's flatter plane was all the rage, his mercenary approach to strategically dissecting a course, or that hunched-over putting stance we grew to know and love. Although Tiger is certainly making an effort to match him, Jack may have rammed home more important putts using that familiar stroke than anybody in history.

But that stroke was bizarre by anyone's standards—bizarre and ingenious at the same time. The Nicklaus stroke is a fold stroke in most ways—one arm powers the stroke while the other arm supports the club and keeps the face square—except for the position of the left arm.

The left elbow is bent almost 90 degrees and is lightly anchored against the rib cage. This moves the left wrist close to the left side of the chest, which in turn requires a more bent-over address position just to get the clubhead to reach the ground. As a result, the left arm is shortened so much that it's about half its normal length. That makes an open stance almost a requirement; it's hard to keep your balance any other way. Also, that open stance means you have to move the ball position forward, closer to the left foot.

That just leaves the right arm to pump that club back and through like a piston. Of course, the left arm is so short now that it can take a lot more force to stroke the ball than a regular fold or pop stroke.

I can see two possible advantages to this variation. One is that it may feel more solid, especially on a windy day, because the body presents such a small area of resistance.

The other advantage is that you may find it easier to aim this way. The lower head position, coupled with

Ruthless Putting

the forward ball position, puts you more behind the ball and may give you a better view of the line. Also, the left arm is so short that the path can't vary much from side-to-side during the stroke.

The claw poses a similar situation. The grip dictates how the arms move (I'll mention it again in the grip chapter); unless you're very flexible, the right elbow will have to bend somewhere during the stroke. And putters using the claw do tend to aim well.

But there are problems with both as well. First, you're *hitting* the ball rather than stroking it. It can be hard to develop "touch" with a stroke like that, and it can take a lot of practice to maintain. And it may require more power to use, making it harder to follow Principle 3

The wrists are certainly more involved in the fold stroke than in either of the other strokes we've discussed so far, but the wrists do not provide power during the swing. **Let me repeat that, with emphasis: THE WRISTS DO NOT PROVIDE POWER DURING THE SWING.**

(keep the grip light). But Jack was positively deadly from ten feet in, as are many claw users, and it *is* possible to use such strokes *with touch* for short putts like that. That's a topic for the tempo chapter.

Of course, all strokes can have problems with Principle 7 (avoid a rigid lower body). But the Nicklaus stroke is more likely to have them because of that extreme crouch position. And if you've got a bad back... ooh! Not good.

Nevertheless, I think the Nicklaus stroke is sheer genius and possibly the most successful stroke the game has ever seen. It's a unique twist on the fold stroke, and it worked very well for him. But some weekend golfers might find the Nicklaus version of the fold to be a little too much work; the standard fold stroke is very efficient on its own, and some putters might find the claw to be a viable alternative.

Then again, if you don't mind a little extra practice, Nicklaus racked up an incredible record with that little fold stroke...

8 The Pop Stroke

I'll be spending more time on the pop than on the other three strokes for one simple reason: Nobody seems to think it's worth discussing. About the best you'll find concerning the pop in most golf instruction is that it was a decent stroke back when greens were not as smooth as they are today, and that the stroke is hard to control and unreliable.

I disagree on all counts. Forgive me if I take a few moments to sing the praises of the much-maligned pop stroke.

I suspect more tournaments have been won and lost with the pop stroke than any other. One of the most successful putters in history, Bobby Jones, was a pop putter. (Most people list Billy Casper, among others, but he didn't pop the way Jones did. You'll understand soon enough.) I don't think you can throw out a stroke with such a pedigree just because it's no longer cool to like it.

It may even be the easiest way to putt, although it can drive players nuts when it goes bad. After all, nobody spends any time trying to understand its strengths and weaknesses.

Trust me, it has both. But so do the other styles. Huggers can be plagued by excessive movement. (Just watch a hugger on a day when their stroke goes south and you'll see a complete meltdown.) Shruggers can get so tight that distance control is impossible, despite the supposed elimination of those tension-causing wrist muscles. (My own theory is that shruggers are more likely to get the yips because they expect their stroke to be so much better than the rest.) And folders can lose directional control just like anybody else.

Ruthless Putting

The pop has its problems, but they're not as bad as most people think. It's not a technically perfect stroke by today's standards, but it's surprisingly dependable once you understand its mechanics. Best of all, those mechanics are very simple. A popper with any sort of game is going to pick a lot of pockets before reaching the nineteenth hole.

Some say pop putting developed because of poor greens and that it no longer suits our super-slick modern greens. I say a stroke that can hole a putt on a rough green is certainly capable of holing a putt on a smooth one. I'll grant you that super-slick greens, such as one might find at Augusta National, require a very soft touch, far softer than you would ever use on a rough green. But Bobby Jones, our pop-putting model, described his action as *sweeping* the ball across the green. And correct me if I'm wrong, but didn't Bobby Jones have something to do with Augusta?

The biggest problem with popping is that *virtually no one knows the proper way to do it!*

We're going to fix that problem over the next few pages.

Don't believe the naysayers when they tell you that no good putter will use the pop stroke. I'm going to show you how to prove them wrong.

Remember: Poppers usually keep the right arm slightly bent and use the left hand and arm to power the stroke. The wrist of the right arm is used as a hinge, not a power source.

For comparison purposes, I'll refer to the incorrect method of popping as the "standard pop." If you don't see the word "standard" in front of it, I'm talking about the properly-done pop stroke.

Faux Popping

One reason the pop stroke has such a bad rep is because of a simple misunderstanding: *The wrists do NOT provide the power in a properly-made pop stroke.* Such a stroke can work but it's very high-maintenance, not the sort of thing that interests a weekend putter.

A second misconception is that a popper locks both arms against his body. This may be necessary in a wrist-powered stroke; otherwise the path of the putter is very difficult to control. But the pop stroke, like the fold, utilizes independent arm motion. The popper rests *only one arm* against his body; the other moves freely.

The Pop Stroke 55

If you're trying to visualize this, you can easily see why the pop stroke is unlike any other stroke. Huggers and shruggers use their arms as a single unit; even the folder's arms can both move freely. But the popper is different: One arm remains fairly stationary, lightly anchored to the body while the wrist acts as an unpowered hinge; the other arm provides the motive power to swing the club.

I think you can see why the pop stroke hasn't gotten much attention lately. Between the bad press and the misconceptions—and the fact that the arms don't work as a unit, which is the current fad—it appears to be more trouble than it's worth. It's ironic that two of the most popular solutions to putting problems these days are essentially pop strokes using specialized equipment. (I'm talking about belly and long putters, of course.)

Before you rush out and buy one of those specialized putters, grab your regular putter and give the pop stroke a try. Believe it or not, the pop is nearly a true pendulum stroke, easy to execute and easy to control. And it's not all that difficult once you know its secrets.

Let's look at the techniques used by the master of this arcane knowledge—the oldest teacher in our panel of experts, Bobby Jones.

The Bobby Jones Stroke

Bobby Jones was the idol of Jack Nicklaus and, like Nicklaus, he played the game on his own terms. He still influences generations of golfers with the filmed lessons he made back in the '30s, but his putting stroke has been all but ignored.

It's easy to see why. It looks like something from the twilight zone of putting.

Jones might disagree with me when I call his a pop stroke, but it fits the general definition I gave earlier—one arm and wrist forming a stationary hinge, the other arm providing power. But what most players would call a "standard pop" is based on the mistaken assumption that the left arm is anchored. Jones anchors not the left arm but the *right* arm. If the standard pop were a rifle, the Jones pop would be a catapult. The standard pop tries to minimize motion; the Jones pop is an elaborate display of graceful motion.

Once you try the Jones stroke, you realize his description of it as "sweeping the ball across the green" isn't just a metaphor. My comparisons of the two strokes

Ruthless Putting

indicated that the clubhead can move up to ten inches more in the Jones stroke than in a standard pop. That allows the stroke to be much longer and lower, the way our Basic Principles say it should.

To be more specific, the standard pop has one pivot, located at the left wrist. The Jones pop has *two* pivots—one at the right wrist, the other at the right elbow; and the *elbow*, not the wrist, is where the anchor point is. Then the left arm pushes *down and back* to swing the club. This double pivot is what enables the pop stroke to have that low takeaway, as recommended in Principle 6.

But it gets better. Have you ever seen a teacher on TV (or had a lesson yourself) where the student was given a ball and asked to toss it underhand toward the hole? This is generally done to help the student gain an idea of how to "feel" the distance to the hole. It's a great lesson... except nobody really putts that way.

Unless you putt like Bobby Jones, that is.

Try it—no ball necessary, just try to get the feel of this move. Face your target, let your right arm hang by your side with your open right palm facing the target. (If you bend your elbow 90° so your forearm is parallel to the ground, your palm should face up.)

Now, lower your arm back down to your side, palm toward the target. *Gently rest your upper arm against your side.* Your elbow will be at about waist level and it will feel almost like your elbow is resting on top of your hip. Keep your upper arm in place and lift your forearm slightly; your open palm should be no more than six inches ahead of your hip.

Now it gets interesting.

With your arm in this position, place your putter in your right hand. Leave enough room at the top of the handle for your left hand, and make sure your right thumb is on the flat part of the handle.

Imagine an aim line running from right to left in front of you, with the hole on your left. Open your left side about 45° (an open stance) with no more than six inches between your feet. (This is how Jones stood.) With your upper right arm still in position, let your hand turn enough so your palm faces the "hole"; the clubface should be square to the aim line now.

Try making a few practice swings this way, just holding the putter in your right hand. DON'T TRY TO COCK YOUR WRIST; JUST LET THE WEIGHT OF THE CLUBHEAD SWING FREELY. Anchoring the elbow prevents your arm

The Pop Stroke

from moving a whole lot, but this should feel similar to the original tossing motion.

Here's what you should feel: Your wrist will cock and uncock of its own accord as you move your forearm. The swing will feel slow and graceful, as if you were sweeping

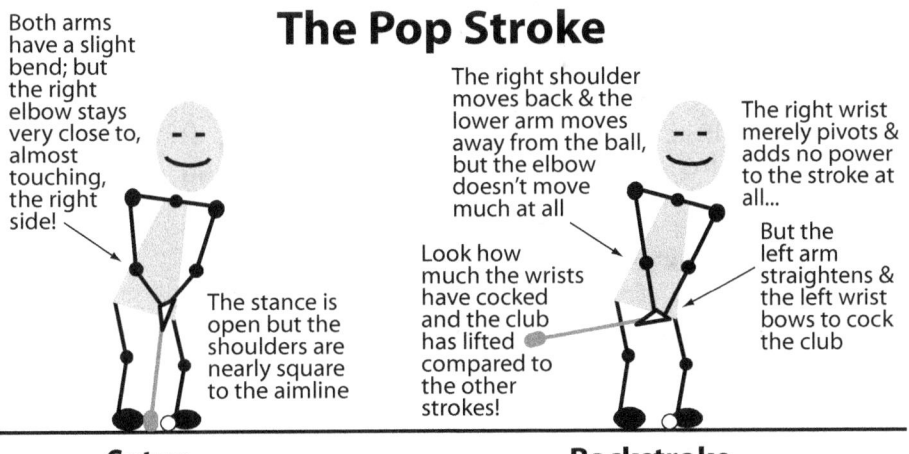

The Pop Stroke

Setup — Both arms have a slight bend; but the right elbow stays very close to, almost touching, the right side! The stance is open but the shoulders are nearly square to the aimline

Backstroke — The right shoulder moves back & the lower arm moves away from the ball, but the elbow doesn't move much at all. Look how much the wrists have cocked and the club has lifted compared to the other strokes! The right wrist merely pivots & adds no power to the stroke at all... But the left arm straightens & the left wrist bows to cock the club

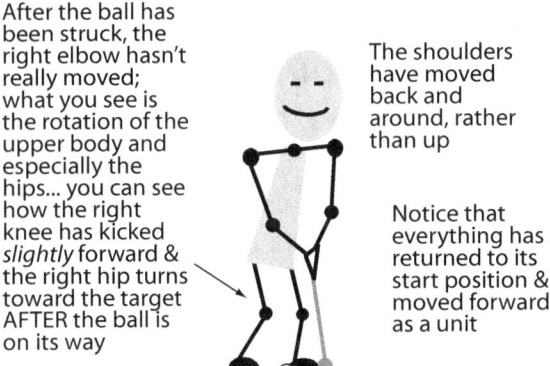

Followthrough — After the ball has been struck, the right elbow hasn't really moved; what you see is the rotation of the upper body and especially the hips... you can see how the right knee has kicked *slightly* forward & the right hip turns toward the target AFTER the ball is on its way. The shoulders have moved back and around, rather than up. Notice that everything has returned to its start position & moved forward as a unit

ball position shown for reference

with a short broom. You might be surprised at just how long and low the stroke is, and how smooth it feels.

In a lot of ways, this stroke is darn near genius.

If you put your left hand in place on the handle you'll find that, while the motion to swing the club back is a bit unusual, you don't have to do much on the

Ruthless Putting

downswing except try not to interfere. Your left arm will straighten, and your left wrist will move through about 45°. (The drawing exaggerates how much the club swings up going back; I wanted to emphasize the wrist cock.) It's a motion that appears far more complicated than it actually is.

Well, it's pretty simple once you make the mental adjustment. See, you may tend to use your right hand to power the stroke... Jones used his *left* hand. Yes, you read that correctly. The right hand serves as an unpowered hinge and, while it has the flexibility to move as much as ten inches, it actually only moves three or four... at most. The left hand does the bulk of the maneuvering here.

In his writings Jones notes that he did like to give the ball a "tiny flick" with his right hand, just as he made contact (BJOG 85). This could be interpreted as wrist-power, but I suspect it's just a slight firming of the wrist at impact. During my own experiments with the Jones

> **An interesting side note: Jones appears to have used almost the same motion for his chip shots and short pitches as well. If this stroke appeals to you, you may find yourself with a built-in short game.**

pop stroke, I noticed a tendency to roll the right wrist at impact; tightening my grip a little did help stop it.

The popper can also have aiming problems. Jones occasionally had trouble with his left hand (the power hand) moving the club off its intended line. (I should mention that I didn't have this problem; I suspect this had to do with the way Jones gripped the putter, which I'll discuss in a moment.) His solution was to bend his left elbow slightly and point it toward the target. This placed the motion of both arms in the same plane, and he said it was as near a panacea for his problems as he could get (BJOG 83-64). He also recommended playing the ball forward in the stance, off the left toe (BJOG 90).

The Jones stroke is a valuable stroke to experiment with, even if you don't intend to use it. Most of you won't need to open your stance a full 45°; something closer

The Pop Stroke

to 30° will probably work just fine. However, I found it difficult to get the Jones version of the pop to work well from a square stance; the pivot point of the right elbow is just too far away from the aimline, and moving the elbow to the front of the body changes the mechanics.

An interesting side note: Jones appears to have used almost the same motion for his chip shots and short pitches as well. If this stroke appeals to you, you may find yourself with a built-in short game.

And *that* certainly appeals to a weekend putter... three for the price of one!

(About that aiming problem: Jones held the club in the fingers with his grip, while I use the "lifeline" grip recommended in the Basic Principles. I think that's why I didn't have the aiming problems that prompted Jones to point his left elbow toward the target. However, I suspect he used the finger grip to avoid a dramatic change in feel when chipping or pitching. You might want to try a finger grip as well if you want to try building a complete short game from this stroke.)

Concerning our Seven Principles: The most likely problems I found were with Principle 5 (while I never developed a cut stroke during my experiments, a hook stroke is a distinct possibility) and of course Principle 7. As I have said repeatedly, all of us have a tendency to get rigid in the lower body, but the pop requires more leg movement than most strokes. That's because the elbow is anchored to the player's side.

So those are the four strokes. No matter what your current stroke looks like, it probably resembles one of them. You can use what you've learned so far about the mechanics of each stroke, along with the Basic Principles of Good Putting, to help make your stroke do its job better.

But wait, there's more! Stroke mechanics aren't the whole story. There are other things that affect your ability to putt well, aspects of putting that you may never have considered because they seemed so simple.

As simple, for example, as how you grip your putter.

9 Why Your Grip Matters

If putting were only about the action used to make the stroke itself, golf would be so much simpler; you would choose the stroke you liked best, and away you'd go to putting mastery.

But it's not that simple. The pros spend hours each week working on their putting strokes, only to have them fail at critical moments. They consult teachers, mental coaches, possibly even shamans, warlocks, and witches in their attempts to gain some sense of consistency from round to round. (Well, there's *some* superstition involved, that's for sure.)

Perhaps a change of grip is all that's really needed.

Principle 3 says that the club should be held lightly and with as little tension as necessary. And Principles 2 and 4 refer to the hands working together… but they mean more than that. The grip we use to hold the club affects the way we stroke with the club.

Or, to put it more bluntly, the grip *changes* the stroke. If we want to make a good stroke, we'd better be sure we've chosen an appropriate grip.

Remember when you look at the pictures in this chapter that they are taken from the putter's left side (as though you were standing at the hole) and show how a righthander would grip the club. You can use a mirror to see how a lefthander would do it.

The Rationale Behind Grips

Obviously, my take on grips is very different from what you may have heard. I agree with the Seven Principles, of course; the first four tell what a grip should do. But saying what a grip should do is not the

Why Your Grip Matters

same as saying *how* it should do it. Supposedly all grips follow the Principles; supposedly all grips will allow you to hit the ball in the intended direction with the correct speed.

But why should I choose, say, a reverse-overlap grip instead of a crosshand grip?

None of our experts give an answer for that one. Utley and Jones prefer a reverse-overlap, and Pelz doesn't have a preference (although he recommends players try a crosshand if they don't have a favorite grip already). Assuming a grip fulfills the demands of the Seven Principles, comfort appears to be the main reason most players choose a grip.

Comfort is good. I like comfort... but a grip that feels uncomfortable at first can become very comfortable with a little use.

The question remains: Why choose one grip over another? Is there a reason that has a bearing on how I get the ball into the hole?

Indeed there is.

All grips, no matter how plain or exotic they may appear, are created for one of two purposes: Either they

> *All grips, no matter how plain or exotic they may appear, are created for one of two purposes: Either they **en**courage the hinging of the wrists during the stroke, or they **dis**courage the hinging of the wrists during the stroke.*

*en*courage the hinging of the wrists during the stroke, or they *dis*courage the hinging of the wrists during the stroke.

That's it... no more, no less. Grasp this one principle and you hold the master key to understanding the bewildering variety of grips out there. The reason there are so many different grips in the first place is that there is more than one way to achieve each of these goals.

Wrist Flex: Putting Disney-Style

Although Pelz allows that a bit of wrist hinge is acceptable (PB 298), he adds that most good putters

Ruthless Putting

say they putt best on the days when they hinge less (PB 48). Of course, he seems to believe that using the wrists automatically causes the little muscles of the hands and arms to take over and affect both direction and distance... but especially distance. He discourages any but the slightest amount of wrist flex.

Utley seems to side with Pelz, allowing a slight amount of wrist flex.

Jones used his wrists quite a bit in his stroke. Not surprisingly, he encourages freedom in the movement of the wrists.

And me? I find myself musing about... *Disney animatronics.*

Yes, I'm thinking about all those robots that litter the landscape of Disney theme parks.

And no, my mind isn't wandering.

I once saw a two-hour special on the History Channel about how Disneyland and DisneyWorld were designed and built. They talked about the technical problems involved in creating things like the Tree of Life at Animal Kingdom and the Tower of Terror at MGM. But none of these problems stumped the imagineers (that's the Disney name for their designers) quite the way the animatronics did.

You see, a large part of Walt Disney's dream involved creating realistic figures to interact with visitors to the parks. The key word here is *realistic*. It's one thing to make a robot that looks like a human being.

It's another thing entirely to make it *move* like one.

You see, human movements can be duplicated quite easily with motors and servos and hydraulic cylinders and fluid; that's no problem. The problem is the *speed* of the movements. There's a lot of force involved in these motions, and the movement must be done slowly in order to control it.

Walt Disney wasn't satisfied with that. He wanted both speed *and* control. And his people worked on the problem for years before they finally solved it.

The Disney imagineers use the term "compliance" to describe their solution. For example, let's say you raise your hand to catch someone's attention. Your hand doesn't move to an exact spot and then stop; it actually moves slightly past the spot where you intend it to stop, then *it snaps back*. We see this motion all the time, so we don't really notice it. But once the imagineers discovered it, they were able to make their animatronic characters

Why Your Grip Matters

move as quickly as they wanted and still control their actions.

If you try tossing a ball underhand, you can see this compliance at work. The motion is slow enough that, if you pay attention, you can actually feel your wrist move slightly past the point where your arm stops on the backswing, then repeat the motion at the point of release. You don't normally notice these movements because they're unconscious; you're not *trying* to do them, they just happen.

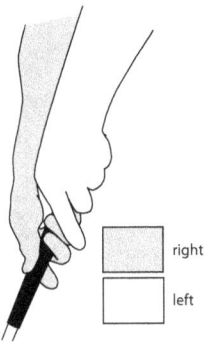

Reverse-Overlap Grip

right
left

And then we pick up our putters and try to eliminate this wrist movement in the name of control. The Disney imagineers would say we were crazy!

I can guess what you're thinking. "Complaince is control *with speed*. I don't need speed in the putting stroke—my stroke is too quick as it is!"

But I don't think we can solve the problem of quick strokes until we have control *with speed*. Ask any sports psychologist—heck, ask any parent—and they'll tell you the fastest way to worsen a problem is to say "no!" Once we start telling ourselves not to move so fast, that we have to slow down, we make speed the focus of our attention. If you knew you could control the putter even if you got a little fast, would speed really be such a problem?

That's why compliance is such an important concept for us… and compliance in the putting stroke is mostly a matter of wrist flex. We don't want to be thinking about wrist flex ("Oh, I need to let my wrist hinge right *here*"); it's something that should just happen on its own.

And that's why we choose one grip over another. Some strokes require a lot of wrist movement while others require very little. If you choose a stroke meant for limited wrist flex but use a grip that allows a lot of wrist movement, you're just asking for putting problems.

What we need to do is match the grip to the stroke. One thing you'll notice is that there is more than one way to achieve compliance; if you think of compliance as a shock absorber working at the change of direction, you may find the concept easier to grasp.

Ruthless Putting

We should also take a few moments to talk about extremes of wrist movement. For example, you'll repeatedly hear teachers talk about keeping your wrists from "breaking down"—what Pelz refers to as "floppy wrists."

But neither do we want to commit the opposite sin. We don't want our wrists to be stiff and immovable.

If you watch a great putter like Ben Crenshaw you'll often see what appears to be a small wrist cock on his backswing and a slight movement forward at the end of the followthrough. This is NOT a breakdown of the wrists. Rather, it is a *wrist flex*. What is the difference between stiff wrists, wrist flex, and breakdown?

A breakdown is a complete failure of the wrists to maintain control of the putter—the complete opposite of stiff wrists, which result from trying too hard to keep the putter under control. Again, a true wrist flex is more like a shock absorber, allowing the clubhead to come to a gentle stop at either end of the stroke.

This flex is a vital component of that ephemeral thing we call "feel"; if you try to eliminate flex from the stroke, you will find it very difficult to control your speed and distance. I'll return to this concept in the tempo chapter.

Ten Finger Grip

right
left

Understanding how much flex a stroke is designed to have is simple enough:

Strokes where neither arm bends during the stroke tend to keep the wrists more quiet throughout the stroke; strokes where one arm bends during the stroke will also cause the wrists to flex more at some point in the stroke.

Makes sense, doesn't it? Neither arm bends during the hug and shrug strokes, so the wrists will tend to remain firmer throughout those strokes. Likewise, one or both arms bend during the fold and pop strokes, so the wrists will have to flex more during the stroke.

We can be a bit more specific than that, however.

Extremes

Our modern experts lean toward a "firmer" grip. The club is in the palms, forming a relatively straight line with the forearms—basically, the putter is an extension of those forearms. This is clearly meant to improve

Why Your Grip Matters

directional control; a lack of forearm rotation, combined with minimal wrist bend, should minimize any tendency to move the clubhead off-line. I believe it's safe to say this is the primary motivation, although they'll certainly say that the longer "pendulum" thus formed makes distance easier to control. (I'd say the jury is still out on that one. If it were true, the pros wouldn't be so widely separated in their putting abilities. Their full swing skills aren't nearly as different, despite the greater number of levers at work. They generally hit the ball pin-high with their irons, yet routinely hit putts several feet past the hole.)

Jones, on the other hand, seems more motivated by the "feel" aspect which affects our ability to control distance. Granted, greens may have been slower back in his time. But Augusta National, home of the Masters and Jones's pet project, has always had fast greens and Jones had no problem there.

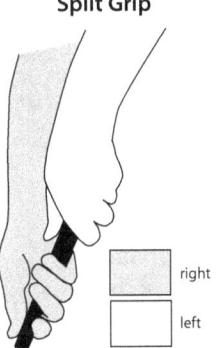

Split Grip

right

left

Jones incorporated a lot of wrist cock in his stroke. His assessment of his own putting was that he was best at distance putts and had to work out ways to keep the club on-line.

I wonder if these aren't really the two extremes of the putting stroke, rather than a balanced approach.

Now don't get me wrong. There is *nothing* wrong with an "extreme" approach. There are essentially two variables in the putting stroke, distance control and directional control. Choosing an approach that minimizes or eliminates one of these variables entirely so we only have to worry about the other seems to show considerable wisdom, if you ask me.

Still, I wonder what a more balanced stroke might look like... Surely it would exist somewhere between these two extremes, between firm wrists and freely-hinged wrists.

We'll call this median move a compliance swing, and we'll use that gentle underhand toss motion as a guide.

Your hand, wrist, and forearm will most likely be relaxed. Your wrist will likely bend backward, just slightly, as your arm finishes its backswing. And as your arm moves forward, the wrist will move back to its original position and then continue on toward the target as the

Ruthless Putting

arm's forward motion eases to a stop and the ball is released.

Of course, there will be no rotation of the forearms; the wrists will flex in one plane only.

Could such an ideal movement be made with a club? It would certainly be more complex; the club is longer and heavier, and the grip requires both hands rather than one, complicating the mechanics of the movement. In addition, the wrist may need to flex three-dimensionally as we are now swinging around our body, rather than in a straight line. (Well, maybe not you shruggers...)

The grip proposed by our modern teachers would seem well-suited to this stroke; the "grip-along-the-forearm-line" eliminates some of the complexity of the movement while still allowing a slight flex in the wrists.

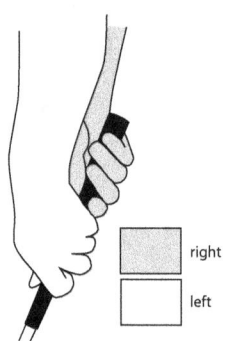

Crosshand Grip

right
left

But the Jones move isn't so bad either. He apparently intended to make the putting stroke as much like the full swing as possible, maybe to gain some extra consistency in the stroke. And while he used what I think was a pretty large wrist break, the pop stroke doesn't demand it by any stretch of the imagination.

I suspect any stroke could incorporate this ideal move without much trouble. The modern approach would require slightly less arm swing since the added wrist flex would provide a bit more power. The Jones approach, on the other hand, would require slightly *more* arm swing since there would be less wrist movement. Less wrist movement certainly lessens the chance of accidental forearm rotation, so some of the Jones problems with directional control should be eliminated.

Is this truly an ideal stroke? I don't know, but it's certainly more mechanically sound. Again—and I know I'm running this in the ground, but it never gets talked about enough—this slight flex shouldn't be thought of as a wrist cock to get more power, but rather as a shock absorber, or maybe a braking motion, to make the club's change of direction smoother. It has the effect of *slowing* the clubhead speed, allowing more control over distance without violently changing the clubhead's direction.

Why Your Grip Matters

With all these thoughts in mind, let's take a look at some of the options we have when we grip a putter.

The Basic Grips

Despite the wide variety of grips available, I've chosen to show only four. They are the reverse-overlap grip, the ten finger (or baseball) grip, the split grip, and the crosshand grip (also known as "left hand low"). Believe it or not, almost all grips resemble one of these.

Certain putting styles work better with certain grips. The shrug requires the firmest wrists, then the hug, then the fold. The pop needs—in fact, *requires*—the most flexibility in the wrists.

The common grips, from firmest to most flexible, are the crosshand grip, then the split grip, and then the ten-finger grip, The reverse-overlap is the most flexible of

Strokes where neither arm bends during the stroke tend to keep the wrists more quiet throughout the stroke; strokes where one arm bends during the stroke will also cause the wrists to flex more at some point in the stroke.

all, which shouldn't be a surprise, as the reverse-overlap was developed when pop-putting was all the rage.

I should add that the crosshand grip can be done as a *reverse-overlap crosshand*, a *ten-finger crosshand*, or a *split crosshand*. Of these, the split crosshand is the firmest; and the ten-finger crosshand, which is probably the most common, is slightly less firm. I can't see any reason for using a reverse-overlap crosshand, but it would be the most flexible of the three.

(We've already mentioned the *claw* when we covered the fold stroke, but here's the detail on the grip itself. As unusual as it looks, it's merely a split grip with the right hand fingers *on top* of the handle instead of under it. The unusual position of the wrist makes the claw more than just firm; it's positively *rigid!* Because of this, I'd have to rate it as the firmest possible grip; but be aware that this extreme rigidity comes at a price. The

Ruthless Putting

claw is virtually devoid of feel, which means you need a lot of practice to play well with it. That's why I haven't included a picture nor given it more space here.)

A good grip needs to provide feel and stability. Some of the grips give more feel, and some more stability, but I believe all four provide an good compromise of both.

Here's a quick summary of these common grips:

- *The reverse-overlap grip is the most used but I think it's the least satisfactory unless you're a pop putter. Most players using this grip would probably be better served by the ten-finger or split grips.*
- *The crosshand grip is a good grip if your putting style is built on firm wrists. (Many of these players might be happier with a split grip. In fact, the split grip is the most underrated grip in golf.) Anyway, the crosshand is best suited to the shrug and nearly useless with the pop.*
- *The ten-finger and the split grip are essentially the same, the difference being that the hands touch each other in the ten-finger grip and are separated (sometimes by several inches) in the split grip. However, this minor change can make a huge difference in how much flex they allow. Think of that split as an adjustment; the ten-finger grip allows slightly more wrist flex, while the split grip is firmer.*

Let me add one more thought here, this one from Dave Stockton. He says that some people improve their putting by turning their left hand slightly *stronger* on the handle. (That means they turn their hand so that the left thumb is pointed more to the right; now the palms aren't parallel to each other anymore.) By changing the plane in which the wrist flexes, it firms up the left wrist without tensing the muscles. Try it on your own putter and you'll see how it works. This gives you yet another way to adjust the stiffness of your grip.

Based on this knowledge, we can also make some general observations from which to begin matching a stroke to a grip. We'll start with the extremes.

- *The pop stroke and the reverse-overlap grip are a match made in heaven, because you need maximum wrist motion in this stroke. The ten-finger grip also works well; being a bit firmer, it can help keep the pop from "getting away from you." The split*

Why Your Grip Matters

minimizes feel somewhat, and the crosshand is almost physiologically impossible to use.
- On the other hand, the shrug stroke works extremely well with the crosshand and split grips, because these two are meant to reduce wrist motion. I like just a bit of wrist motion when I shrug, so I generally use the ten-finger grip. The reverse-overlap is really poorly suited to the shrug; it requires a lot of conscious effort to keep the wrists firm throughout the stroke.
- The hug can work with almost any of the grips; it all depends on how much wrist movement you find acceptable. Personally, I like the ten-finger or split grip with this stroke; the crosshand really stiffens the wrists, and the reverse-overlap can easily become more of a popping motion.
- As for the fold… well, that all depends on your version of it. The fold can be blended with any of the strokes and, as I said earlier, it often is; pure fold strokes are rare. Because of that, the fold can work with any of the grips. For example, my fold is more of a pop-fold, so I tend toward the reverse-overlap or the ten-finger, depending on how I feel that day.

And that brings up one last thought on grips:

I know most teachers advise sticking with one grip, and that's good advice when you talk about the full swing. But is that good advice for a putter?

Because most of us use flat-sided putter handles on our clubs, all four of these grips are essentially the same hand positions; the main difference is how far apart the hands are, so it's not a major change to switch between them.

Have you considered changing the position of your hands for different length putts?

Some people make more short putts using a stiffer grip than normal; have you considered a split grip for short putts? Jones said he was a much better lag putter than a short putter; perhaps you would be a better distance putter if you changed to a grip that allows more wrist flex as you get farther from the hole.

Or maybe it works the other way round for you. I, for example, tend to use *more* wrist flex on short putts; I can use a shorter stroke that way, and with my technique, the putts stay on line better.

This is a very personal matter, but learning how much wrist flex is comfortable for you can have an immediate

Ruthless Putting

effect on how well you putt from different ranges. It just amazes me that more players don't experiment a little to find out what works.

Wrist flex is such a normal and necessary part of the putting stroke that it's nearly impossible to avoid it. This is a case of what you don't know *can* hurt you, because unintentional wrist flex can ruin an otherwise consistent swing… and leaving out necessary wrist flex can destroy it as well.

10 The Gravity of the Situation

This chapter may well be the most important in the book, as it deals with that illusive thing known as *feel*.

How long does it take to develop feel? How much work is required? Is there some magic training aid or surefire practice routine that will deliver results? And most importantly, once you've got it... how do you hold on to it?

Most believe feel to be a fleeting thing, like catching the wind. And yet, for those who are willing to listen, feel is a natural thing—easily gained, and easily kept.

Why then do we struggle so much? Simply because we can't believe it's so easy. This key to feel has been ignored for literally decades, despite being part of the Basic Principles agreed on by virtually all teachers.

Principle 6 says "The putterhead should travel on a long low path, as close to the ground as possible, both going back and through." *But why?* Why must the putter head travel a long low path, as close to the ground as possible? Is it just a matter of keeping the ball on line, as many would have you believe?

No, it's not. This long low path is the result of the technique that provides feel in the putting stroke. Listen to me carefully:

You don't need metronomes or hours of practice to make a good putting stroke. Forget rhythm; think *swing*. If you learn how to swing the club, you can go to the green, make good strokes with your favorite putter, pick up a friend's putter of an entirely different length and weight, take three or four practice swings, and be able to make a good stroke with it. (Your aim may be off if the putter doesn't fit you, but you will swing it like it's

The Way of the Putter

an old friend.) If you know how to swing, your rhythm will adjust automatically.

Let me say that again: *If you know how to swing, your rhythm will adjust automatically.*

For some of you who are fighting yips, learning how to truly swing the club may make them magically disappear. Even if they don't, work on the material in this chapter because it will lay a solid foundation for the section devoted to curing yips later in this book.

In his short film **How I Play Golf: The Putter**, Bobby Jones ended his lesson with this quote:

> "Well, just remember that long backswing and you'll find that your putts always go up to the hole. Never, never feel like you're hitting the ball—just a nice long sweeping stroke."

Earlier in the lesson Jones is even more direct: *"What I like to see is a long, smooth, unhurried stroke which literally sweeps the ball along the green."*

This may be the least understood teaching from his entire series. In this age of the power game, Jones's words are generally considered bad advice.

Take a shorter swing and accelerate through the ball; that's the word for today. Strike it firmly enough to propel the ball 18 inches past the hole if it doesn't go in. Spend hours on the practice green to groove an accurate stroke. Set a goal—make 100 putts in a row before stopping, for example—to build a sense for putting under competitive pressure.

Contrast this with Jones, who wrote:

> *"A backswing that is too short goes inevitably with a grip that is too tight. No one ever stabs or jabs a putt when the club is held gently, and the arms and legs are relaxed; but always something goes wrong when he drops down on the club, crouches low over the ball, and hits it sharply, with the idea that he won't give the face of the club a chance to come off the proper alignment"* (BJOG 84-85).

Or this:

> *"There are, of course, good putters among the so-called average golfers who by patience, study,*

The Gravity of the Situation

and practice have developed putting methods they follow as they would a ritual; on the other hand, these instances are rare. Anyone who hopes to reduce putting—or any other department of the game of golf for that matter—to an exact science, is in for a serious disappointment, and will only suffer from the attempt" (BJOG 88).

According to Charles Price (BJOG iv-xv), Jones spent no more than three months a year playing golf, including his travel time to and from tournaments, and often went for months without so much as picking up a club.

Imagine that. For nine months each year—nine months!—Jones spent most of his time doing things other than playing golf, and then played himself into shape for three months of competition. Yet he, a mere amateur, routinely bested the pros of his day. And this was no small thing, because he played against pros like Walter Hagen, who won five straight PGA Championships... at match play!

He did this using a putting stroke that not one modern teacher recommends. I want you to think about that for a moment. He basically *relearned* how to putt each year with an unusual stroke... and *won* each year as well.

Surely this man wasn't just talented; he *knew* something we don't. And since he was both a lawyer and an engineer (read that as "a man predisposed to logic and mechanics"), I tend to believe the latter.

And much of it was tied up in these words at the end of his putting lesson: *"Well, just remember that long backswing and you'll find that your putts always go up to the hole. Never, never feel like you're hitting the ball—just a nice long sweeping stroke."*

What is Jones saying here? In a word, the key to feel is **gravity**.

A Weighty Concept

Could it really be that simple? Is it really possible to control a putt with gravity?

Bobby Jones seems to have believed so. Modern teachers want us to hit the ball, but Jones wanted us to use gravity and *sweep* the ball.

Try this little experiment. Take a golf ball. Hold it out at shoulder height... and drop it. Do it several times, and just pay attention. Now answer one question:

The Way of the Putter

Did the ball fall at a constant speed, or was it accelerating? (I'll give you a hint; it's a trick question.)

Drop it a few more times if you need to, and try to answer again. Constant speed or acceleration?

If you don't *know* the correct answer, you probably can't even guess it. Chances are you think it looks like it's falling at a constant speed, but somewhere in the back of your mind you remember your high school physics teacher saying gravity was an acceleration.

In fact, *gravity is a constant acceleration*. Gravity is measured at 32 feet per second per second, normally written as 32 fps^2, which means the speed increases at a rate of 32 feet per second every second: at 0 seconds, the speed is 0 fps; at 1 second, 32 fps; at 2 seconds, 64 fps; at 3 seconds, 96 fps; and so on. Because we see it every day of our lives, we don't usually think much about it. Our minds generally register it as a constant speed; we don't have much else to measure it against.

> *"Well, just remember that long backswing and you'll find that your putts always go up to the hole. Never, never feel like you're hitting the ball—just a nice long sweeping stroke."*
> **What is Jones saying here? In a word, the key to feel is gravity.**

Why is this important? What does it have to do with the Jones putting stroke? Permit me one more digression; I think it will all make sense then.

On pages 53 and 54 of his book ***Jim Flick on Golf***, Jim Flick tells of a study Dr. David Williams made on some film of Bobby Jones's swing made during the '30s—around the same time as the film series ***How I Play Golf***. He wanted to make some measurements of Jones's swing as he hit a ball about 250 yards. The measurements showed that his clubhead was traveling about 113 mph, which compares very well with the major pros of today (most of them are in the 110-120 range), and is especially impressive since Jones was using a hickory shaft.

But as impressive as that was, perhaps more impressive was his hand speed. You would think that his hands were absolutely flying around his body to

The Gravity of the Situation

achieve that kind of clubhead speed. But, in fact, his hands were only traveling about 34 fps^2—barely above the acceleration of gravity!

Think about that. Jones was basically *just dropping his hands* to create that massive clubhead speed.

You're probably ahead of me now. If that's what he did when he drove the ball, why wouldn't Jones do the same thing in his putting?

"Well, just remember that long backswing and you'll find that your putts always go up to the hole. Never, never feel like you're hitting the ball—just a nice long sweeping stroke."

That's exactly what he did. And he taught it on a grand stage—the Warner film series—so an entire generation grew up hearing about it.

Why isn't it taught today?

I suspect part of the reason is technology. When steel shafts replaced hickory, much of the swing theory that had evolved earlier was dropped in favor of "fresh ideas" based on the new technology.

Part of it was probably the new heroes who came along and exploited the new technology. Byron Nelson and Ben Hogan immediately come to mind; both spent time mentoring others, and of course Hogan wrote books like **Power Golf** and the legendary **Five Lessons**.

Just as importantly, the full swing was what the new shafts revolutionized most. Putting became less emphasized, and with players like Hogan and Snead being, shall we say, "less than enamored" with the game on the greens, putting was viewed as less important.

And let's face it, as cool as it might have been to be a great putter, they weren't the guys winning the most tournaments... at least not until Nicklaus came along. And Jack, like his hero Bobby Jones before him, didn't do things the way everybody else did. He reshaped the full swing with that upright move and flying elbow, and he reshaped the putting stroke with that deadly accurate piston stroke of his. Both were well-suited to a "steely" competitor like Jack... and both took a lot of practice to maintain because they were muscle-powered, unlike Jones's gravity-powered game.

It's no wonder that when science finally approached the putting stroke, it focused on the well-muscled modern style.

I'll give Dave Pelz credit for getting oh-so-close to the gravity game. On pages 138ff of **Dave Pelz's Putting**

The Way of the Putter

Bible he suggests finding your personal "body rhythm" and using this to help find your putting stroke speed. He likens this rhythm to that of a pendulum, the swing rhythms of which are controlled by their length and weight.

I'm not going into the physics of pendulums; Pelz certainly knows more about them than I do. But I have a problem with his solution to the rhythm problem. On pages 227-230 he suggests what he calls the "touch-touch" drill—swinging a putter back and forth between two pillows in a "tick-tock" cadence in conjunction with a metronome until you find a comfortable, low energy rhythm. (I give Dave credit here because, conceivably, the rhythm that used the least of your energy is getting most of its energy from gravity.)

I'm sure that this drill helps many people. If you don't have a good understanding of how gravity affects a putting stroke, and if you have trouble stroking putts in a consistent manner, anything that smoothes out your putting rhythm is a blessing.

But this drill will neither teach you the feel of a gravity stroke nor give you the relaxed control possible with such a stroke.

Why?

Because it ignores the real heart of a gravity-fueled stroke.

How to Get a Hold on Gravity

Way back in the dark ages—before Woods, before Nicklaus, even before Hogan—the predominant way to move a golf ball down the fairway was to *swing* the club, not hit with it. This was, as I said earlier, largely a function of hickory shafts; the things had so much flex in them that it was well nigh impossible to muscle the ball around with them. Walter Hagen was one of the few successful "hitters" of the era, largely because of his incredible short game.

At the time, a common way to teach the feel of a swing (still used by some teachers like Jim Flick, Bob Toski, and Manuel de la Torre) involved tying a small weight (traditionally, a penknife) to the end of a string and trying to swing it gracefully from a waist-high backswing to a waist-high followthrough, back and forth. This helped the pupil develop a smooth swing by ingraining the feel of gravity—after all, if hickory was flexible, string was positively limp and impossible to muscle around.

The Gravity of the Situation

This is still an excellent method to learn the feel of a full swing.

Or a putting stroke.

Try it. Seriously... it's important. Any old string or twine will do, but I realize that twine isn't a common household item anymore. Try an old shoelace—the thinner, the better. If you use string, cut a piece about 2½ feet long and tie a small weight to the end. (Penknife optional; any small weight, like some old keys, will do. If you have to use a thicker shoelace, just add more keys.)

Your Training Aid: An Old Shoelace and Some Keys

Now, take hold of the end without the weight, using both hands as though you were holding a club. Take your putting stance and start swinging the weight back and forth. Try to swing it so that the string and weight stretch out straight from your hands, so it looks as if you were swinging a real putter with an incredibly skinny shaft. Don't be surprised if it's a bit difficult to start the motion; it takes a few swings of your arms and hands to get it going.

One thing you'll find out quickly is that it's difficult to make the "club" swing with just your wrists; the forearms need to move as well. (That's one reason why the Jones pop stroke works well when other pop strokes don't. At the risk of sounding like a broken record: The wrist may hinge, but it doesn't power the stroke.) This helps not only with your putting stroke but your full swing as well; it teaches you to swing smoothly with arms and wrists, and not just jerk the handle.

It's frustrating, isn't it? Can you believe you have to swing the "club" so slow to mimic the action of a real club? (The paradox here is that, even though it feels terribly slow, it really develops quite a bit of clubhead speed. Remember, Jones says you'll never have a problem getting the ball to the hole.) The real frustration comes at the extremes of the swing where you change direction, doesn't it?

Try to feel that change of direction. Remember when you were a kid on a swing? Remember how it felt when you reached the top of your backswing, at the top of your "stroke," just before you started back down? You could feel yourself slowing, slowing... then you just hung in midair for a moment, weightless, before your weight settled back down on the seat and you swooped down, gaining speed. You zoomed through the bottom of the arc then up, slowing, slowing, then weightless again, almost like you were going to fly out of the seat. (If you were like me and ever tried to jump off the swing at the top, you learned that you had to jump *before* you reached this point of weightlessness or it was too late; you pushed out of the swing but dropped straight down to the ground. All forward momentum was gone; you were literally just hanging in the air.) And then you felt your weight on the seat again, and the whole speed-up process began again…

Do you feel that sensation when you swing the little weight at the end of this string? Can you feel that moment when it coasts to a stop and hangs weightless in the air before reversing direction?

If it continues to elude you, perhaps you have too much tension in your wrists and forearms. Remember back in the grip chapter when I spoke about the need for some flex in the wrists? Don't *try* to flex them; just *allow* them to flex if they want. Try to relax your forearms so much that your wrists can flex a little *even though it's only a weighted string*. They won't flex much, if at all, but just the attempt to relax should be enough to let you feel that moment of weightlessness. Once you can feel this tiny pull, it's an epiphany; *this is feel!* The fingers, hands, and forearms are more sensitive than you might expect.

This is the key to your putting stroke. Not the back and forth tick-tocking motion of some personal rhythm, not some mental metronome tick-tick-ticking in your head… but that brief moment in time when the clubhead feels weightless during your stroke. Get where you can feel that consistently (it doesn't take long), and you'll have 90% of the feel and tempo puzzle mastered.

This is how Bobby Jones regained his touch so quickly year after year despite not playing much.

Continue to work with your weighted string. Try different length swings; try to feel the moment of weightlessness at the extremes of the stroke.

Now get your putter and hold the end of the string against the grip so you can swing them together. That's what you want to do—make the weighted string and the putter swing in the same rhythm, so the shaft and the string stay parallel with each other. Allow your wrists to flex if they want; it will be more pronounced now.

The Gravity of the Situation

(I know what the physics-minded among you may be thinking. If the rhythm of a pendulum is determined by its weight and length, as Dave Pelz said, shouldn't the weighted string and the putter have different rhythms? Don't worry about it. You're not worried about the rhythm, you're concerned with the feel at the change of direction... gravity will affect them both the same way. The problem comes if you swing the putter too stiffly, and using the string with it will help you avoid doing that.)

Now try to duplicate that feel using only the putter. You don't have to hit balls at this point; all you want to do is feel that change of direction. Remember: *The wrists may flex slightly*. It may take some time to feel it, but be patient. It's worth it.

If you have a copy of it, go back to that **How I Play Golf** short again. Watch Jones putt. Time after time you'll see that putter "hang" in space just before it starts smoothly down to meet the ball. *"What I like to see is a long, smooth, unhurried stroke which literally sweeps the ball along the green."* Can you see the motion? More importantly, can you *feel* it as you watch? If so, you can actually practice your stroke just by watching Jones putt.

Can you say *visualization*?

And as if that weren't enough, I bet that you can instantly recall this feel anytime you forget it just by repeating the little experiment we did at the beginning of this chapter—that is, dropping a golf ball from shoulder height. This time, just listen for the ball to hit the ground. You won't believe it until you try it, but the time from release to sound is almost exactly the same as the time from change of direction on the backswing to ball contact.

Try it. It's amazing!

Why do I keep harping on this? Why do I want so badly for you to feel this?

Because *gravity is a constant acceleration*. Think about what that means.

All modern teachers agree that distance control is most important factor in putting. The phrase you'll hear over and over is "speed determines line." The trick is to gain speed control, even when you're tense or nervous or tired...

None of these things affect gravity. Gravity accelerates the putterhead at the same rate on the 18th green at the Masters on Sunday afternoon as it does on the 1st green at the local muni on Saturday morning. It doesn't

The Way of the Putter

care whether you're playing at sea level at Myrtle Beach or high in the Rockies. (Well, at least that won't make a noticeable difference in your swing.) It doesn't care whether you're excited or bored.

Learn to use gravity when you putt, and your speed control will be remarkably consistent over time. You'll use less effort and you won't be tempted to force things, so your overall performance will improve.

True, there will always be some muscle interference when you putt. It can't be helped, if for no other reason than you have to *hold* the club. But if you're concentrating on that moment of weightlessness rather than how much the putt might mean, your muscles won't interfere very much. (Hey, automatic help with Principle 3. Hold that club lightly, kid!) You lose yourself in the moment, in the doing of the thing... modern sports psychologists

> *The trick is to gain speed control, even when you're tense or nervous or tired...* ***None of these things affect gravity.***

call this "process vs. outcome" or some such psychobabble. But no matter what you call it, it's unusual because this feel creates a "swing mechanic" or technique of its own, an even rarer thing in golf because virtually everybody feels this sensation the same way.

A universal feeling, recognized by all. Amazing...

Amazing that this small thing should be so important to the stroke. Still, I guess it shouldn't surprise us. The force of gravity still perplexes the greatest scientific minds among us. It's a force we grow up with, that affects us in profound ways, and yet we tend to ignore it as we go about our daily business simply because its effects are so common.

At the risk of boring you, I'll repeat myself yet again. Learn to feel this weightlessness at the change of direction, the smooth acceleration that starts the downswing, and you'll begin to hit your putts straighter because you won't jerk the putter off-line as much.

Your contact with the ball will be more consistent because you won't move so much over the putt.

Your distance control will improve because, given the same green speed, a backswing that moves the ball

The Gravity of the Situation

two feet today will feel the same as a backswing that moves the ball two feet tomorrow.

You'll develop a grip with less tension.

And your confidence will grow, because you'll know instantly if you're stroking your putts correctly.

"Well, just remember that long backswing and you'll find that your putts always go up to the hole. Never, never feel like you're hitting the ball—just a nice long sweeping stroke."

Jones understood the gravity of the situation. You should too.

A Final Thought: Stroke Flexibility

What's amazing to me is how much of Jones's writings consist of suggestions rather than rules. For example, in the book **Bobby Jones on Golf**, Jones will give a range of setup options and the explanation that he used this one yesterday, that one today, and maybe another tomorrow—all depending on which felt more comfortable. "The stance can vary considerably, shifting the feet to favor a hook or slice; the ball can be shifted about within ample limits with respect to the feet. These little changes are by no means fundamental. Even what might didactically be prescribed as the correct swing allows some latitude in these matters" (BJOG 212).

Therefore when one of the greatest golfers of all time, who seems to believe that most golf technique is somewhat fluid, repeatedly states without qualification, "Nobody ever swung a golf club too slowly" (BJOG xii), maybe we should pay attention. A slower stroke is a flexible stroke, one that allows our natural abilities to unconsciously adjust for the little daily differences in how we feel.

When your stroke becomes almost self-correcting, you're well on your way to mastering your putter.

11 Why Can't I Aim?

There are always new training devices for sale that are guaranteed to straighten out your stroke or improve your aim... for a price.

You can get hi-tech devices with lasers, and devices that read every little nuance of your stroke and give instant feedback.

You can get low-tech devices that clip on the face of your putter, devices that mechanically guide your putter path, and devices that you place in front of your ball and putt through.

You can buy impact tape for the putter, fake holes for the green, and blocks of foam for wedging your forearms apart.

You can even stick a couple of pencils in the green and tie string between them... or just stick a tee in the ground and try to hit it.

Far be it from me to disparage any golfer's attempts to improve their putting. Some of us find that a device, regardless of how sound or how bizarre its working theory may be, helps us make progress. Maybe it's the extra bit of hope that each new toy gives... or just the determination to prove to ourselves that we didn't waste our money.

But with all the devices and such that have hit the market, we still struggle with greens reading. No teacher likes to admit it, but the truth is this: You can hit the ball with all kinds of screwy strokes and still get the ball to go in the hole... provided you started it on the right line.

Reading greens is probably the hardest putting skill to master.

Why Can't I Aim?

Why does it have to be that way? All we have to do is look at the green. Everything is right there in front of us.

Dave Pelz has done a lot of research on this problem. (As he has on most aspects of the putting game—big surprise, right?) He has discovered what I think is a fascinating fact: Most of the break in a putting green is actually *invisible*.

Ok, maybe I should say invisible to *the conscious mind*. Pelz says that our subconscious mind can sense it and cause us to make unconscious adjustments to our stance and stroke in an effort to get the ball on line. He also says that most putters only see about a third of the break; they unconsciously adjust for another third in their setup, and for the final third with their stroke. Even then, they don't adjust enough; it's not unusual for players to miss on the low side of the hole.

Furthermore, Pelz says it's difficult for players to learn to aim for the actual break because, even after we learn to set up on the correct line, our minds continue to subconsciously adjust for the unseen break. The result then is that all putts are missed high, and the player gets frustrated and goes back to their old way of putting before their minds can adjust to the corrected aim.

It seems that reading greens is a losing game, one that drives all golfers nuts. If we want to improve, it looks like we'll have to change our way of *thinking* about it.

Pelz wasn't the first to discover our tendency to underread break on a green. Bobby Jones wrote about it decades ago:

> "There is one thing a golfer should always remember and always practice. In any round there are always numbers of times when the proper line to the hole is obscure; if it were always visible, we should miss few putts. But it is always a good practice, when the correct line cannot be determined, to borrow generously from any slope and to attempt to cause the ball to pass a tiny bit above the hole." (BJOG 99-100)

Pelz believes we should strive to eliminate all of the unconscious compensations we make during the putting stroke, but I don't. I agree that it's a good idea to limit how much adjustment our minds have to make, but I think *great putters allow some unconscious adjustment*. As I will point out in the yips section, some things should not be under conscious control if we want to excel. Our minds are *built* to work that way.

Think about throwing a ball underhand to someone. You don't count off how many paces you are from them. You don't take measurements of how high their hands are above the floor or above (or below) your own hands. Even if they're moving, you can generally put the ball close enough that they can catch it easily. Our brains do this sort of calculation all the time… and do it well.

There are even more variables in putting, many of which we can't account for even if we consciously know they exist. Our minds account for most of them anyway. We shouldn't hesitate to use this skill to the utmost!

> *I agree that it's a good idea to limit how much adjustment our minds have to make, but I think **great putters allow some unconscious adjustment**. As I will point out in the yips section, some things should not be under conscious control if we want to excel. Our minds are **built** to work that way.*

I agree with Jones and Pelz that we can improve our putting drastically just by assuring that the ball is on the correct side of the hole. Then our minds can "do their thing" and make the necessary adjustments to get the ball in the cup.

Perhaps I should explain this concept in more detail. Let me quote a bit more of the Bobby Jones piece I referred to earlier. Dave Pelz says the exact same thing in his book, but Jones is briefer:

> *If the ball remains above the hole, there is always a chance that it will fall into the upper side, and it is certain that it will at any rate stop not far away. But once a putt begins to roll below the hole, every inch it travels carries it farther from that precious cup. (BJOG 100)*

That's simple enough, isn't it? When the ball comes down the slope toward the hole, it's approaching the

Why Can't I Aim? 85

top or highest side of the hole and the entire hole is open to it. But if the ball is coming in from the side or bottom (which frequently happens when we underread the break), the chances of it going in are greatly reduced and, once the opportunity is gone, the ball continues its merry journey *away* from the hole.

The top is the "correct" side of the hole because it offers the best chance to make the putt. You may also hear it called the "pro" side of the hole because the pros will try to make sure that, if their putt misses, it misses on the side that gives them the best chance of making it.

But Pelz's research indicates that the number of putts missing on the low side greatly outnumbers those missing on the high side, even among professionals. And the reason, as stated earlier in this chapter, is that virtually everybody sees only one-third of the actual break.

Pelz's solution, obviously, is to play three times more break. I have found that to be difficult, partially because you need to pick your target near the hole. I tend to pick my target much nearer to my ball position or, when I can see the line clearly, by looking at the apex of my line. I don't know if the distance between the apex and the hole changes my perspective or what, but I simply can't get comfortable over the putt. As a result, I actually tend to putt worse.

I've been studying the Pelz research, as recorded in his **Putting Bible**, and I think I may understand why. What you're about to read in the remainder of this chapter doesn't contradict any of his findings, but simply interprets them a little differently.

Pelz says the subconscious mind continues to make unneeded compensations even when you play more break, and needs a lot of practice to get used to the new setup. I think I've also discovered the reason for that, and I believe the mind will adjust just fine once it understands what is being changed.

I know this chapter may seem very elementary to some of you, but it's important that your mind grasp both what the ball normally does during a putt and how an aim change affects the putt's path. Therefore, what follows is a step-by-step explanation of the physics of a rolling ball. Don't worry, there are no long technical terms or involved mathematics involved. We're just going to examine, one at a time, the forces that affect how the putt rolls, and then we'll add them altogether until we understand:

Ruthless Putting

- *why a putt breaks,*
- *what that break looks like, and*
- *how we aim to achieve that break.*

But before we do, I want you to understand that, no matter how meticulously you analyze data and develop techniques, reading greens will always remain something of an art. Straight putts are easy to read, but Dave Pelz estimates that less than 2% of all putts are straight (PB 146). Does that mean the remaining 98% have a simple break that can be easily read? I doubt it. Few greens are built like flat tilted planes with a single consistent break along the ball's desired path. As the putt gets longer, the likelihood that you're dealing with a compound break causes a simple formula like "allow for three times the visible break" to become less and less useful. At best, we hope to eliminate three-putting from our game. Keep this caveat in mind as we try to understand the behavior of balls on the green.

The First Force: Gravity

To simplify things a bit, we're not going to start with a putt but with a ball falling through the air.

If we hold the ball out to our side and drop it, it falls straight down to the ground. Simple enough; but be sure to take note of this fact: The ball started falling *just as soon as it left our hand*. It didn't hang in the air for a second; it just *fell*. Boom. Like that.

You think I'm belaboring the point, I can tell. (I'm psychic like that. It goes with being a writer.) Well, you're right; I am. It's far more important than you think. Remember this fact: *Gravity affects the ball immediately the moment it's released.*

Now let's take it a step further. We'll load the ball into a small cannon aimed *parallel* to the ground, and we'll shoot the ball out of it. What happens to the ball now?

The Second Force: Launch Velocity

The ball shoots out of our cannon with a constant horizontal velocity that we'll call our *launch velocity*. It's a constant speed, unlike the acceleration of gravity, and it covers the same distance during each period of time we measure.

Although there are now two forces acting on our ball and its trajectory is determined by the combination of these forces, each force acts independently of the other.

Why Can't I Aim?

This means that gravity is still working on the launched ball just as it did on the falling ball; as soon as the ball leaves the cannon, it begins falling immediately, no matter how much horizontal velocity it has. The launch velocity only keeps it from falling straight down, just as gravity keeps the ball from travelling perfectly parallel to the ground.

Also, because gravity is accelerating the ball toward the ground, the ball now falls in a curved shape that gets steeper as the acceleration increases. If the ball doesn't hit the ground and the launch velocity doesn't run out, eventually the ball's trajectory will become almost (but not quite) vertical.

The Third Force: Friction

But the launch velocity *will* run out. The air creates friction around the ball, and this resistance will eventually slow the ball's horizontal launch velocity to zero. Then the ball's trajectory will become completely vertical. (The air friction will also prevent gravity from accelerating the ball forever; when that "terminal velocity" is reached, the ball will continue to fall straight down at that now constant speed.)

The addition of the friction force gives us the traditional trajectory we're used to seeing.

Launch Velocity Plus

Of course, we rarely shoot balls out of cannons; we usually throw them. And we don't generally throw them horizontal to the ground because we'd have to throw them really hard and they *still* wouldn't get very far before they hit the ground, which really takes the fun out of most games.

Instead, we toss the balls *upward*. And when we do, things happen pretty much the same way they did with the horizontal toss.

When we toss the ball upward, we give it a "straight line" velocity not unlike the cannon's launch velocity—only the straight line isn't horizontal, but angled upward. This "launch line" is affected by the same forces as before; gravity still causes the ball to drop below the "launch line" just as soon as it leaves our hand, even though the ball continues to move upward because the downward acceleration of gravity slows its upward launch velocity. When gravity finally slows the upward motion to zero, the ball begins to turn downward at a point we call the

Ruthless Putting

"apex" (marked with an 'A' in the following diagram) and we now see a trajectory that looks more familiar to us.

Then it gets *really* interesting.

If we draw a line from the "launch point" (the hand of the tosser in the diagram) to the apex, notice two things:

- *The line from the hand to the apex is a much lower line than the launch line.*
- *The actual path of the ball is above the apex line at the beginning of its trajectory (that's the gray area), then it crosses back below that line as it passes through the apex.*

Did we need any of this knowledge in order to learn how to toss a ball? Of course not! We learned it by trial and error, *subconsciously*, and now we don't need to think about these things if we should suddenly want to toss something to our friend on the sofa over there. And since we usually looked at the target we were tossing to, rather the apex of our toss, our brains learned instinctively to *launch the ball above the apex*.

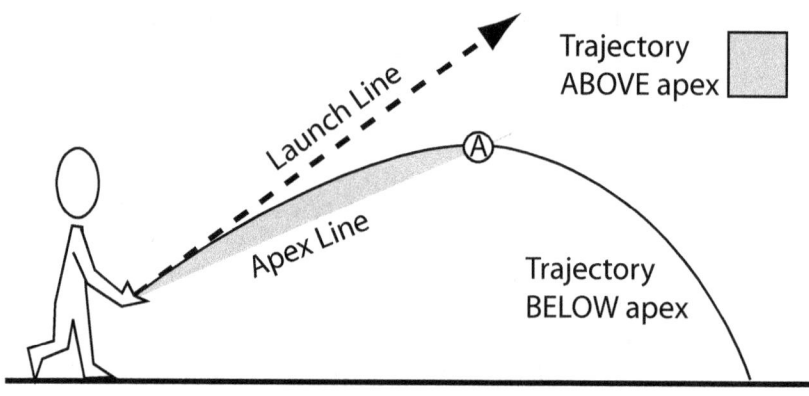

Tossing a Ball Through Its Apex

To use Dave Pelz's term, we just let our brains make *compensations* during the toss.

Off To The Green!

Now let's head off to the putting green. We come upon a breaking putt like the one on page 89 (as seen from our putting stance): A lot of things are easily transferred from our earlier example—the ball, the apex

Why Can't I Aim?

of our trajectory, our target (the hole), the launching force (the putter stroke), friction (the surface of the green)...

STOP RIGHT THERE. What's wrong with this picture?

This is where I think Dave Pelz misses an important part of the puzzle. He says his "pure-in-line-square" stroke is like other sports motions, and on page 84 of his book he pictures four "strokes" from other sports—croquet, bowling, basketball, and pool—that he also says are "pure-in-line-square." But his logic is faulty here for one obvious reason:

*In all of these sports, the trajectory of the ball is **in the same plane** as the "stroke."*

Not so in golf. The trajectory isn't in the same plane, nor even simply perpendicular to the plane; it's at an acute angle, and that angle isn't the same every time. Even if you develop the vertical stroke that Pelz teaches, only straight putts will conform to his ideal and, as stated earlier, less than 2% of all putts are straight. The rest will be at varying angles, depending on the slope of the green.

And those of us who don't swing as Pelz teaches (and I think it's safe to say that includes a lot of us) will find that *all* strokes are made at an angle to the trajectory of the ball.

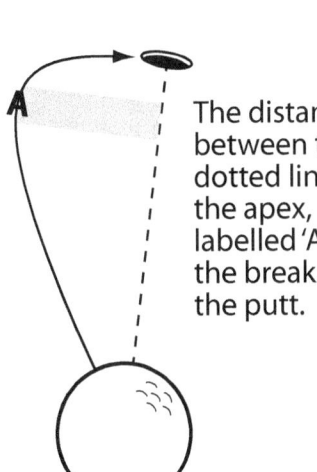

The distance between the dotted line & the apex, labelled 'A', is the break of the putt.

Because of this, *our minds can't interpret the trajectory the way it's always done.* Instead of just factoring in things like gravity and friction, now there are compound angles affecting the launch as well as our view of the trajectory. This means we can't aim in a way familiar to our brains. We're used to looking at the target while launching the ball straight upward; now we typically look at the apex as well while launching the ball on an inclined plane where the speed of gravity combined with surface friction changes from hole to hole. (That's a fancy way of saying the green speed changes.)

What's the only aspect of our mind's previous experience with trajectories that clearly transfers to this new playing field? That's right—it knows that the ball should be launched *above the apex*. However, in this new situation, the ball must be launched *to the side of the apex of the trajectory.*

And so, through trial and error (our mind's ever-faithful method of learning), we learn to start the ball out to the side above the apex and let it drop back through the apex toward the hole. (Bear in mind again that, in the traditional vertical orientation our mind is used to, dropping the ball through the apex is the same as aiming the ball directly at the target.) All told, it's quite a marvelous accomplishment.

There's another repercussion of this attempt to launch the ball on a trajectory that's on an inclined plane. Pelz notes on page 157 that he (like his students) had always erroneously envisioned his putts as going *straight at the apex* and then arcing down sharply. Furthermore, he says it's hard to get people to see the actual trajectory... and this perplexes him.

I can tell you why it's hard. It's because what we *expect* to see is so close to what we *do* see. The diagrams on this page and the next show what I mean.

This first diagram shows what we *expect*; we expect the ball to go straight to the apex and then curve down into the hole. Because we expect this, we won't tend to notice the ball moving to the outside, *above* the apex. It's that unconscious move that, you'll remember, our minds learned to do by trial and error without us really noticing. We've done it that way since we were kids, after all; it's nothing out of the ordinary.

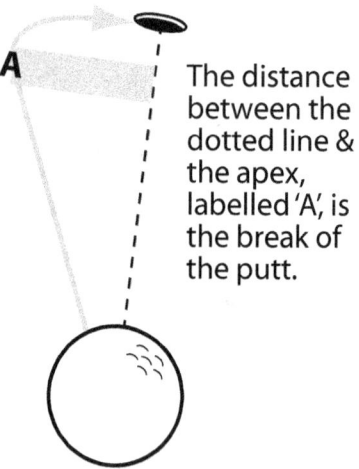

The distance between the dotted line & the apex, labelled 'A', is the break of the putt.

In addition, the line is foreshortened from our point of view. That further influences the apparent sudden break toward the hole at the end. On the next page I've superimposed the bad concept diagram on this page with the actual putt pictured on page 75:

Look at how close the two lines are! Except for the actual trajectory's initial move outside, the two are virtually identical. From my angle of view, *the faulty concept is incredibly close to what I actually see;* so why should I question it? And since my brain has been adjusting for this faulty concept since I began putting, it's not going to change tactics *unless it fully understands why it's wrong.*

Why Can't I Aim?

Is it any wonder we have difficulty trying to improve our putting? Our minds are doing the best they can with an adapted aim system and skewed perspective.

Go over this material several times until you truly understand the problem. Pelz says his students have a lot of trouble getting used to aiming where they want the ball to go without subconsciously hitting the putt outside the intended aim line. The reason is not so perplexing once you understand how closely what is happening actually matches what is *expected* when seen from the putter's viewpoint.

This is what you see when you stand over a putt. The ball is actually following the smooth dark curve; but because of foreshortening, it looks like it's going straight toward the apex, then diving toward the hole like the gray curve.

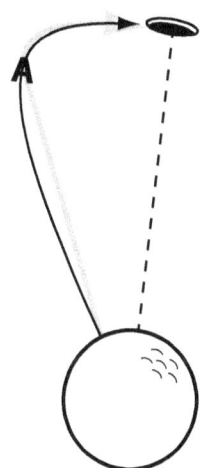

Once you consciously understand what you are unconsciously doing, you can "reconfigure the playing field" so your unconscious mind does what you want. Listen to any pro talk about "visualizing the shot" they want to hit. If you can clearly "see" what you want to do, your subconscious mind will tend to make your muscles move in a way that will cause it to happen.

Now all we need is a way to "see" what we actually want to do. That's the easy part!

Ruthless Putting

Consciously Unconscious Putting

Let's return to that putt diagram from page 89 and add a new line—an aim line that represents where we want to start the ball. I've added a dot labeled 'B.'

I mentioned that I based this on ideas from both Jones and Pelz. Simply put, the Pelz research shows that putts break three times more than we read. That gives me a problem; not because I disagree with him, but because I don't look at the hole when I putt. I tend to look at the apex instead, so that "three times the break" bit doesn't really help me.. (This may also help explain why I've had fewer putting problems; since my target is much closer than the hole, I haven't had to compensate quite as much to get my ball close.) In addition, since the apex is much closer to me than the hole is, foreshortening alters how "three times the break" looks to me, especially on a long putt where I need it most.

After studying the photos in the **Dave Pelz's Putting Bible**, I realized that this "three times the break" finding was based on (or at least, primarily illustrated with) simple flat slopes. Most importantly, all of those slopes were covered with *grids* to make it easier to track the ball's progress to the hole.

This may not sound like a big deal, but think about it. Not only can you see how much break the ball takes as it rolls toward the hole... you can figure out how far the apex is from the hole, *and therefore how close the aim line comes to the apex!* For someone like me, who aims at the apex, this really is a big deal.

As it turns out, the apex on a simple slope is about two-thirds of the way from me to the hole... which means that the aim line is only *twice* the break at the apex. Or, to make it extremely simple...

> *If, like me, you aim at the apex rather than the hole, all you have to do is see how much break the putt has, then aim that high above the apex! If I aim at the point labeled "B" in the diagram, and if I get my speed right, my ball should end up very close to the hole.*

This is a very tidy and very simple method of aiming. I think you'll find it's much easier to double something than to triple it. (Have you ever tried to fold a letter into equal thirds? I think most people would agree when I say it's easier to fold it in half.) And because you're making a

Why Can't I Aim?

smaller adjustment over what you see—basically, you're aiming "one break" above the apex rather than "three breaks" above the hole—and because that adjustment is made closer to you, your brain doesn't have to make as big a compensation, even if it continues to work with the faulty perception that you aim the ball straight at the apex.

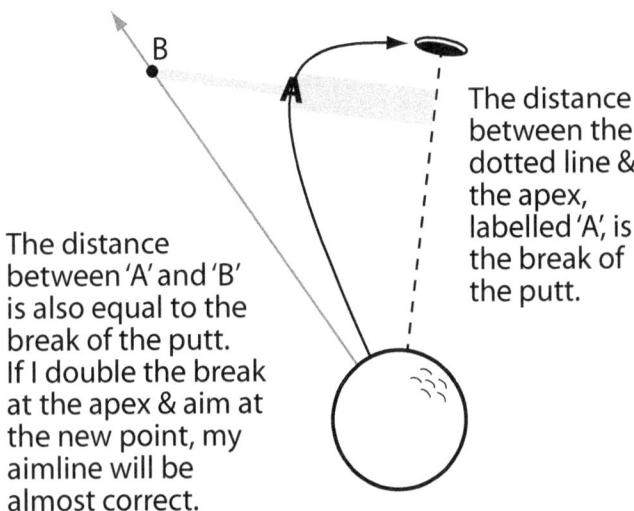

The distance between the dotted line & the apex, labelled 'A', is the break of the putt.

The distance between 'A' and 'B' is also equal to the break of the putt. If I double the break at the apex & aim at the new point, my aimline will be almost correct.

How can you judge your effectiveness at this technique?

It's simple. Just use Jones's idea about "borrowing" a little on your putts. If your putt doesn't go in but misses just above the high side of the hole, you probably got it right. And if it falls just short of the hole but doesn't go too far by, you were probably a little off on your speed. (If that happens frequently, you should probably either take a little longer stroke to gain more speed, or just aim a bit higher. The longer stroke will usually be the simplest of the two.)

And that's it. There's no shortcut to reading greens; you have to deal with different grasses, changing weather conditions, multilevel greens with odd slopes—heck, you even have to deal with grass growing during the round! But if you understand what you're doing and why you're doing it, I bet you'll spend less money on putting aids... and that means more money for greens fees!

12 Fine-Tuning Your Putter

Getting fitted for a set of clubs is a given for most players these days. But have you ever had your *putter* fitted?

You should have... but you can be forgiven if you didn't know that. Far too much of the talk about putters is limited to design and technology.

As it is, you'll hear arguments over face-balanced putters and toe-balanced putters; blades and mallets; specially grooved faces and soft inserts; even back-weighted inertial putters and super-heavy putters. And did you know you can buy a putter shaped like the USS Enterprise from *Star Trek*?

But that's just the clubhead! You still haven't decided whether to get a curved-neck shaft or an standard straight shaft, perhaps dressed up with an offset hosel. And if you want to set off a civil war, just get the purists debating the virtues of forged blades versus the investment-cast variety.

Rather than going into the vast variety of designs available in putters these days (and more will be introduced soon, you can count on it), I'm going to focus on the things that make a putter feel good and aid in making solid contact. You may be surprised at what you read in this chapter but I suspect you'll find it to be pretty accurate, even when you look at what the pros are doing.

There are rules that must be followed, however...

The Rules of Golf, Appendix II

Although they don't change much from year to year, each year the USGA publishes a new edition of **The Rules of Golf**. If you have a copy and turn to Appendix II, you'll

Fine-Tuning Your Putter

see that it lists the guidelines that manufacturers must follow when they build clubs, including putters. In fact, you'll find some spiffy little drawings of putters that show some of the things the USGA thinks are critical. (My drawings aren't nearly as cute, but they get the job done.) Some of the club specs in that appendix don't apply to putters, while others apply *only* to putters. I won't list them all here, just the ones that matter to a fitting.

Club Length

First of all, clubs must be at least 18 inches long. (There is no current limitation on the maximum length of a putter.) Such a short putter would be almost unusable but, as you can see, the USGA tries to cover all the bases when they set their specs.

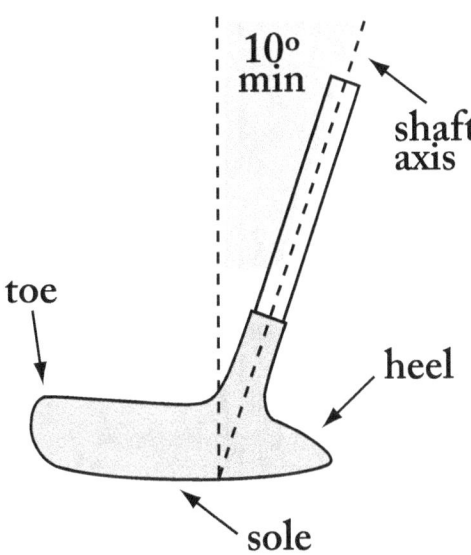

Lie

Lie is the angle between the shaft and the sole of the club (listed at 80° in the rules) and it determines whether the club sits flat on the ground when you set up. The picture shows how it's measured. That 10° angle in the shaft from vertical is required so players can't use a croquet-mallet-type head; the USGA thinks that makes the game too simple. I believe this rule was written because Sam Snead used just a such a putter.

Loft

Loft is the same for putters as it is for other clubs, except a putter can have no more than 10° of loft. (You can putt with any club you want, no matter how much loft it has, but you can't call it a putter if it has more than ten degrees of loft.)

Bent Shafts and Hosels

The shaft of a putter can have a partially curved shaft, or a specially-bent hosel called an *offset* hosel, provided that the bend extends no more than five inches above the sole of the club, and the USGA has some special ways of measuring this that are also set out in Appendix II. Although you have no control over these things (that's why there's no drawing here), some players believe the offset helps you putt the ball straighter. (That's the same logic behind offset drivers.)

In addition, the shaft on a putter can connect to the head at any point, which means you can have center-mounted shafts and such.

Handles

An interesting difference between putters and your other clubs is that putters can have shaped handles like the familiar flattop non-circular handle most of us use. I say this is interesting because most golfers don't realize that it's perfectly alright to use a regular round handle as well. One of my favorite putters has been fitted with a standard jumbo handle, and I enjoy using it quite a bit.

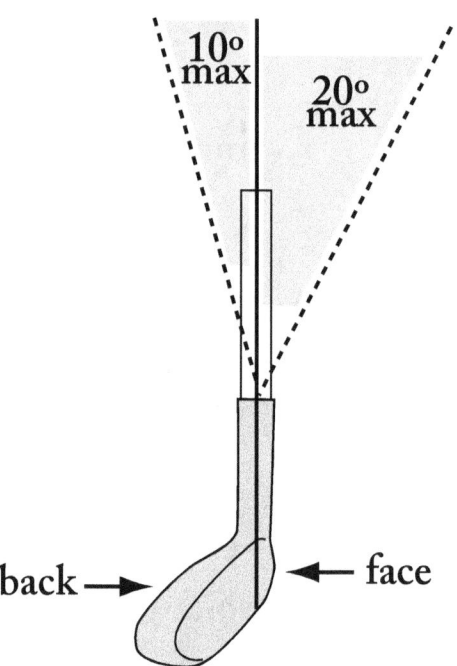

Head Weight and Face Design

There is no limitation on the weight of a putter—at least, not yet. Nor is the texture of the face regulated, so inserts and such are allowed.

Shaft Angle

One other allowable variation of note is that the shaft can lean forward as much as 20° from vertical and backward as much as 10°, as shown in the picture here. This may seem like a strange spec, but Natalie Gulbis uses it. She uses a split grip with an angled shaft that leans forward so she can move the ball back a bit more in her stance, which effectively firms up her grip even more.

Please note: This angle is measured from the top of the hosel, not the little cone-shaped plastic ferrule

Fine-Tuning Your Putter

many clubs have. If there is no hosel—if the shaft enters directly into the head—the angle is measured from the top of the head where the shaft enters.

These are the primary putter design specs that the USGA regulates. How these specs interact with each other determine the playing characteristics of your individual putter.

Face and Toe, Straight and Bent

Despite the bewildering number of putter styles available today, you can divide them into roughly two groups: face-balanced and toe-balanced. You can easily tell the difference if you just hold your putter up in front of you with the shaft horizontal to the floor, one hand near the shaft and the other near the head, and let it rest on one finger of each hand so the shaft can roll freely. The weight of the clubhead will cause the putter to settle so that either the face points straight up—which means the putter is face-balanced—or the toe will point downward—which means it's toe-balanced.

You'll find various degrees of toe-weighting; some will point straight down, but most will point down at an angle. Also, you'll find it doesn't matter how the shaft is mounted. A face-balanced putter may have a straight shaft with a bent hosel, or it may have a double-curve shaft mounted near the heel, or it may have a straight shaft mounted in the center of the head. Toe-balanced putters usually have the shaft mounted in the heel.

The traditional view has been that face-balanced putters are better for shruggers, and toe-balanced for almost everyone else. In my experience, one can feel as good as another as long as the putter is adjusted properly.

I think you'll do better to ignore the standard wisdom and just choose a putter that feels good and looks good when you stand over it. Looks should NEVER be ignored when you choose a putter; a putter that doesn't look right to you will frequently register in your mind as not being lined up properly, causing you to manipulate the club unnecessarily during the stroke. This is another thing for you "yippers" to consider—if your putter looks or feels wrong to you, you may not need a new putter; your current putter may just need an adjustment. (More on that in a minute.)

The main reasons companies use a bent hosel or curved shaft are for face-balancing, as was just mentioned, or to allow offset. As I said, some people believe a little offset will help you hit the ball straighter or see your line better. Both purposes can also be accomplished with either (1) a curved shaft or (2) a straight shaft combined with an extra-long bent or angled hosel.

These are choices you make when buying the putter. Be aware, however, that setting the lie angle of a face-balanced putter more upright may cause it to be more toe-balanced, and flattening the lie angle will possibly make it a bit heel-balanced. This may move the sweet-spot a little toward the toe or heel.

Common Adjustments

The putter specs laid out by the USGA may seem a bit arbitrary, but that's because the real magic is less in the individual specs and more in how they work together. The classic example of this is face angle, which is a major consideration in putter setup *but it isn't even mentioned in the specs*. (We'll look at it later in this chapter.)

Now let's look at some adjustments we can make to fine-tune our putters for our personal putting style.

Handle Size

An adjustment that full-swing teachers are familiar with is handle size. A handle that's too small tends to slip down more into the fingers, encouraging a hook. Likewise, a handle that's too large requires more of a palm grip, encouraging a slice.

This knowledge affects putters as well. If you putt well using a smaller handle, don't change; but if you're having trouble with forearm rotation, you might consider a larger handle. Larger handles encourage you to grip the handle in the palms. This can make it easier to keep the putter shaft in line with the forearms, as well as encouraging a more relaxed grip.

K.J. Choi has been putting very well using a monster-sized handle. You can get one of those, or a large standard putter handle (they come in a vast variety of sizes), or you can use a jumbo round grip like the ones available for your other irons and woods.

Face Angle

Face angle is most easily explained by the diagram on the next page.

When you stand over your putt and look down at the ball, the face of the putter should be square to the line of

Fine-Tuning Your Putter

putt. You could call this a zero degree face angle, and this is what you want. But depending on how you hold the club when you take your stance, the face might actually point slightly to the left or right of the line. (An open clubface seems to be more common than a closed one.)

Face angle is affected not only by changes to loft, lie, and shaft angle, but by hand and ball position as well. For example, you could hold the club so that the shaft looks vertical when you look down at it; but, because the face angle is out of adjustment, the face appears *open*. Someone else might take that same putter and set

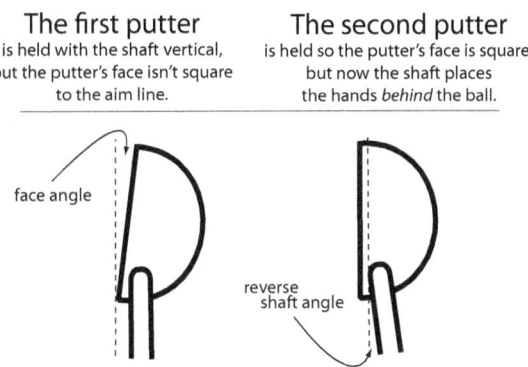

The first putter is held with the shaft vertical, but the putter's face isn't square to the aim line.

The second putter is held so the putter's face is square, but now the shaft places the hands *behind* the ball.

up with their hands *behind* the ball or even behind the clubhead... and the face angle would look square. For that player, the face angle is correct and all is well with the world. Same putter, different setup... different face angles.

Don't take this adjustment for granted. No matter how good your stroke becomes, you're just wasting your time if your putter won't let you use it to full advantage.

Loft

The standard loft on a putter is around three degrees. (At least it used to be; now it varies from manufacturer to manufacturer.) Stan Utley prefers five to six degrees; I thought at first that might be because he uses a flatter lie, but I also like more loft and I use an upright lie.

You may wonder why more loft would be better since the whole idea of putting is to get the ball rolling as soon as possible, not to get it airborne. The reason is that the ball sinks into the grass a little bit and, even if it didn't, the ball skids a little before it starts to roll. A slight bit of loft helps with both problems. It's the same reason you chip rather than putt if the ball is "sitting down" in short rough; the ball is stuck in the grass, so you need more loft to get it "up on top" for it to roll.

Although a putter is manufactured with a certain amount of loft, what really concerns you is *effective loft,* which is a combination of manufactured loft, hand position, and shaft angle. I'll have more to say about this later in the chapter.

Lie

I think lie may be the most critical adjustment you can make in terms of comfort when you putt. A lie that's too flat will put the club up on the toe when you putt and, due to the loft, will make you think you're pushing putts. A lie that's too upright will have the toe up in the air, and you'll think you're pulling putts. It's certainly possible to ignore lie and still putt well—otherwise players like Isao Aoki wouldn't make anything, holding the toe up in the air the way they do—but it's better for your consistency if you set the lie properly.

Some of the lie adjustment machines I've seen show 72° as a standard lie. Stan Utley says he prefers 69°, a little flatter, while I prefer mine much more upright, just a few degrees short of the 80° limit.

Shaft Length

Although you can make do to some extent with a shaft that's a bit too long by choking down on it, shaft length also affects the lie of the putter. Generally you choose the shaft length when you buy the putter, but shafts can be resized or changed at a pro shop.

Of course, some players prefer to have a little extra shaft sticking out above their hands, as this can make the clubhead feel a little lighter during the stroke. And at the time of this writing, Sergio Garcia is apparently using a slightly longer shaft to help him tell when he's flexing his wrists too much. Both are excellent examples of how a simple equipment adjustment can help your swing.

Head Weight

This refers to the weight of the clubhead alone, without the shaft and handle. The weight is usually measured in grams (there are a little over 28 grams in an ounce).

Fine-Tuning Your Putter

The typical putterhead is in the 200-230 gram range, although I have seen some as high as 330. Belly putter heads tend to weigh in around 400 grams, and "broomstick" heads near 500. And, of course, specialized heads with unusual weights are also made.

A heavier head can slow your stroke down and help you "feel" the head better. It can take some experimentation to find a comfortable head weight, some of which you can do in the golf shop. Just try a lot of different putters and see how heavy the heads are on the ones you like. (My local pro shop keeps catalogues that tell the head weights on the different models they carry.)

A good pro shop should be able to make all of these adjustments for you, and it shouldn't take more than a few minutes including the time you need to test them. But you may be wondering... just how much difference do these adjustments make? If my putter seems alright to me, does it need to checked out?

Is it really worth all the trouble?

Why Bother?

During the course of doing putting tests for this book, I found I was having some problems hitting the putts consistently. I finally took some of my putters to a local pro shop and had the lies and lofts readjusted. (Please note: The machine used to adjust putters is a little different from the machine used for your other clubs. Be sure to go to a shop that has the proper equipment.) Perhaps my experience will help you understand just how important adjustments are.

I took four putters with me—a generic Bullseye-style blade, an old toe-weighted Spalding semi-cavityback, a face-balanced Odyssey with a double-bend shaft, and a Nicklaus cavityback. That's a pretty good cross section of what you'll find on most store shelves. And the club tech was a very knowledgeable man who didn't mind answering some questions for me about the sorts of things that can cause fitting problems.

Some putter heads are made from brittle metals, and their hosels can't be bent without breaking. The *faux* Bullseye was one of these; it couldn't be adjusted. It measured in at a lie of 72° and a loft of 3° on both sides. (This is the putter I used to compare left- and right-handed techniques.) I was told that most companies these days consider a lie of 70° or 71° normal; the one used just depends on the company.

Ruthless Putting

The old Spalding was the club which felt best to me. The lie was 76° (very upright, only 4° inside the limit) and the loft nearly 5°. This takes my setup into account; I like to lean the club slightly forward, with my hands directly over the ball. The tech told me that 5° is about right if the greens you play are generally medium to fast speeds; slower greens require more loft to get the ball up on top of the grass.

Also, the bottom of the Spalding is rounded. He told me that some people might think the toe of the club was up in the air but that was an illusion. The area of the face that should make contact with the ball wasn't tilted at all; and the toe, being longer than the heel, had slightly more curve so it appeared to be higher off the ground. (That's something worth remembering.)

> **Please note: The machine used to adjust putters is a little different from the machine used for your other clubs. Be sure to go to a shop that has the proper equipment.**

The other two clubs felt good to me in terms of weight and length, but they didn't feel right at all when I used them. The Odyssey was 7° too flat—seven! imagine that!—and the "lean" angle actually put my hands *behind the putterhead*. (Remember, my preferred setup places my hands *over the ball*.) In effect, I was trying to putt with the club up on the toe and with *negative* effective loft—that is, the loft actually drove the ball down into the grass instead of up on top! Is it any wonder I had trouble making consistent contact?

An interesting note about the double-bend shaft: The technician told me that some of these shafts require special attention for proper bending. Rather than bending the curves to adjust the lie, he took a tool more commonly used to bend the hosels of irons and used it to grip the shaft just above the head. Apparently the shaft on this putter is not inserted into the head, as in many putters; rather, it's fitted over a metal peg sticking up out of the head. If the shaft has a weak spot, it can be broken using the normal tool. He told me a good

Fine-Tuning Your Putter

tech will know when to use which tool. And perhaps because of this knowledge, my face-balanced Odyssey is still perfectly face-balanced. I was certain it would be changed at least a little bit.

The Nicklaus had similar problems, although the lie wasn't off as badly. However, it appeared to be made of a brittle metal and he wasn't sure it could be adjusted without breaking. I decided the club couldn't be used otherwise and we should take the gamble. As it turned out, looks were deceiving; the metal was extremely flexible and it adjusted very easily.

What can you learn from all this?

1. *Find a pro shop with both the proper equipment and a knowledgeable technician. A good tech can anticipate problems and suggest the proper adjustments to achieve the results you're after.*
2. *Make sure you have some idea of the speed of the greens you play (fast greens need less loft), and try to have a consistent setup when you go to be fitted. Both of these affect the lie and especially the loft you need.*
3. *If you're buying a new putter, try to find out if the materials used in the putter are strong enough to withstand adjustments. You'll save yourself a lot of worry later.*

The difference these adjustments made is amazing. Not only do the clubs feel better, the ball actually *sounds* different as it comes off the face. Having your putter fitted is something I can't recommend enough, and it's almost a necessity when you buy one off-the-shelf.

13 Kiss Your Yips Goodbye

Government motto: If it ain't broke, fix it until it is.
—*seen on a bumper sticker*

Yep, that's the story of the yips in a nutshell.

And no, I'm not trying to be funny.

I know this chapter will seem to ramble a bit, but humor me; when we're done, you'll not only know how to beat the yips, but how to keep them from coming back.

Let's demystify the yips once and for all.

Yips Aren't Limited to Golf

When I was in the eighth grade, we had to do some simple gymnastics. One of them was a somersault—you got a running start, jumped onto a springboard, and flipped through the air over a table covered with padded mats. For a kid like me who had never been much of an athlete, it was the coolest part of class and I was determined to get as good at it as I could.

So I started dissecting my vaulting technique. We were taught to use our hands and arms to generate rotation—kind of a mini-spring to help us finish the somersault and land on our feet. So what did I do? I started paying particular attention to the position of my hands when they first hit the table.

I tried to isolate exactly which muscles in my arms contracted to push me up as my feet went over.

I tried to time my pushes to launch me off that table and high into the air, hoping to get a perfectly balanced landing.

And all I succeeded in doing was paralyzing myself. I got so caught up in the details of the movement that

Kiss Your Yips Goodbye

I finally lost the ability to do a somersault at all. The second my hands hit that table, my arms gave way and I crashed into the mats. It was terribly embarrassing.

In the end I managed to do a somersault well enough to get a passing grade. It's just that I had to learn to do it entirely in the air; I couldn't put my hands down on the mats at all. I learned how to hit that springboard and tuck into a little ball so I could rotate end over end as I flew over the table, then land on my feet on the other side.

Several years later I got into the one class every student wants to take—Driver's Ed. The car we learned to drive was a Buick LeSabre, a vehicle so long we referred to it as "the land yacht." And it was *extremely* wide. I guess the school figured if we could keep that thing on the road, we could drive any normal car we were likely to get into.

But it was a daunting task for me. The view from the driver's seat wasn't much different from being trapped in a well. The fenders of the car just seemed to flow over the edges of the lane, and I was desperate for anything to help me keep that monster between the lines.

My key became a small fender-mounted turn signal indicator. From where I sat, that little piece of chrome lined up perfectly with the center line. I just tried to set it on the center line and keep it there.

It didn't really work that well. I kept weaving back and forth between the lines. It just wasn't that easy to keep the indicator on the line, even at a mere 35 mph. I just kept sawing that steering wheel back and forth, and the weaving got worse and worse.

Finally my instructor realized what I was doing (I guess it was a pretty common thing) and told me to forget the area near the car and focus on a spot farther on down the highway. It was difficult at first—I was afraid I was going to jerk across the center line into a truck or something—but was pleasantly surprised to find that I stopped having to correct the car's path so much. Even better, I finally started to relax and enjoy driving.

Why have I spent so much time regaling you with anecdotes from my often-misspent youth? Because both of these stories are classic examples of *the yips*.

I can almost hear your reaction now. "THE YIPS? Are you serious?!?"

Yes, I am... but I'm not surprised you don't recognize them.

Ruthless Putting

There are two things in the golf community that absolutely amaze me:

- *the vast number of golfers who seem to suffer from the yips, and*
- *the fact that none of the teachers offering to help these golfers seem to have the slightest idea what "the yips" are.*

Why did I take the time to tell you these two stories from my otherwise uneventful youth? Because these are not only examples of the yips, but of the two most common ways of dealing with them.

The Cause of Yips

Believe it or not, I hadn't read any of the golf psychology books before starting this book. Most of the things I heard mental coaches say didn't sound much different from two things you learn in a good church—namely, the importance of *character* to the game, which The First Tee has seized onto so successfully, and *faith*. Yes, faith—as in "have faith" in the laws of physics, which are true but don't always make sense ("you must hit down on the ball to get it to go up," etc.) and "have faith" that the habits we have ingrained during practice will serve us well if we will just let go and act.

These are good things for golfers to learn, of course, but I wondered if these guys had anything helpful to say about the yips.

I must say that I was surprised to find that *nobody* seems to know exactly what "the yips" are. For example, Bob Rotella hits all around it, but never quite seems to identify what they are:

> "Putters with the yips... frequently get obsessed with physical factors like whether their left wrist breaks down during the stroke. They do this despite the fact that there is no evidence I'm aware of suggesting the existence of a physical condition called the yips... The yips originate in the mind. Their prevention and cure are mental challenges." (PM 113)
>
> "Players who are immune to the yips tend to be players whose thoughts are less about results and more about process... Players who develop the yips tend to be players who don't understand

Kiss Your Yips Goodbye

that good putting is an uncontrolled, unconscious act. They want to guide or steer the ball into the hole. They try consciously to control their putting strokes, to make them perfect." (PM 114)

"That sort of thinking—the conscious, forceful pursuit of putting perfection—overloads the mind and the nervous system the way turning on too many appliances can overload your house's circuit breakers. Something has to give. When it does, the yips are often the result." (PM 115)

"...the yips are hard to shake once a golfer has them." (PM 112)

Let me clear up this uncertainty right now.

These are not symptoms of the yips; they *are* the yips. Putters with the yips don't just get obsessed with physical factors; obsession with physical factors *is* the yips.

It works like this: You've been putting fine but you've hit a so-called "bad patch." Or you've come up against an opponent who putts lights-out, and you decide you've got to improve to beat him. Or maybe you just want (desperately) to improve.

So you listen to every putting tip you can get hold of. You dissect your stroke. You learn that if your stroke is just one degree off the intended line you'll miss a straight 15-foot putt, so you determine to get that line *just* right. Or you decide you want a missed putt to go 17 inches past the hole like Pelz recommends... or you want it to die in the hole, like Utley or Jones says. So you work to get your speed *just* perfect. Or you hear that for every six degrees your putter's path is off square, the ball will veer off five degrees in that direction, so you work to get your stroke *perfectly* on line.

You become so paranoid about getting things just right that you start trying to adjust things *during* the stroke. You tighten your grip because you can't alter that swinging club unless you've got control of it. You start moving that putter from side-to-side like I sawed that steering wheel during Driver's Ed. You try to adjust the speed as the club comes down the line, but it takes *a lot* of effort... and it jerks the club off its line. You grip tighter. You're so tight now that you can't move forward evenly (and trust me, it's no longer a swing or a stroke, but just a move) so you lurch forward like you're popping the clutch in a Model T.

Ruthless Putting

Your stroke is destroyed. You've got the yips. Bring on the long putter... and a couple of shots of scotch while you're at it. Golf is a hard taskmaster.

Are the yips really that hard to shake? (Ok, bad pun.) They can be. Rotella is right when he says their prevention and cure are mental challenges. But that's all yips are—a bad mental habit—and they can be changed just like any other habit.

Still, some habits are tougher to break than others. Do you want to change? Do you know how to change? If you can say "yes" to both questions, you can beat the yips no matter how tough your case is.

I can't answer that first question for you, but I can sure give you the answer to the second.

Very simply put, yips are the result of *micromanagement*.

> *These are not symptoms of the yips; they **are** the yips. Putters with the yips don't just get obsessed with physical factors; obsession with physical factors **is** the yips.*

That's all. No deep philosophical theories to be grasped, no perplexing medical anomalies... just a futile attempt to control *every* aspect of an action that's supposed to be a loose, free-flowing movement.

Remember what happened when I tried to overcontrol my somersault technique? *I lost it entirely.* Muscle movements that had happened naturally of their own free will suddenly had to be coordinated by my conscious mind... and it wasn't up to the job. What did it do? It shut down. I ended up having to learn another way to get the job done.

Likewise, when I stopped trying to guide the Driver's Ed car perfectly and just focused on where I was going, I stopped weaving and actually started aiming the car where I wanted it to go.

There are two ways to beat the yips. As I did with the somersaults, the first and most common attack is to change your style. Bernhard Langer is the poster boy for this method, having beat the yips no less than three or four times—each time with a new putting stroke—but he proves it can be done. (Also note: Langer proves the yips are a cycle. It's a mistake that can be made any number of times... and also corrected each time. Remember that.)

Why does this method work? The explanation is glaringly simple:

Your brain has no idea how to control the new putting stroke.

Makes sense, doesn't it? You yip because your brain has interfered with the moves your body knows; when you change styles, your brain has new untarnished moves that aren't being micromanaged. Make sure you grasp this concept: *You can't micromanage what you don't know.* Sure, you can start screwing things up again once you've developed some skill with the new style if you insist on micromanaging it... apparently that's what happened to Bernhard Langer.

But take note: Despite apparently making the same over-controlling mistake several times, Langer is still able to putt... *and win.*

The second approach is to change the focus of your putting in a way that prevents micromanagement. That's what I did in Driver's Ed. By looking far down the road, the car seemed to move around less; less movement meant fewer corrections (or over-corrections, if you prefer) and a smoother drive. Ironically, I gained *more* control over the car when I stopped trying so hard.

In either case, you beat the yips by "rewiring your brain." The concept is simple: *Frustrate your brain's attempts to control the stroke until the brain gives up.* This isn't as difficult as it may sound.

I agree with Rotella on this point: You can't practice your way out of the yips; you have to change your attitude (PM 116). You must, as he says, "go back to the mental fundamentals of good putting" (PM 117). But, like others who don't really understand what the yips are, that's all he can say... and that's no help at all. You can try to change your thinking; maybe it will work, maybe it won't. But if there's no real plan of attack to follow, you just have to stumble around in the dark and hope you find something.

That's crazy. Either yips can be beaten or not. If they can, there's a way to do it. If not, then don't hold out false hope.

There *is* a way to do it. I know because I've beaten them. As well as I've putted in my life, I went through a period where I got the yips. I over-analyzed my putting

Ruthless Putting

stroke until I couldn't make a smooth stroke to save my life. Once I realized what had happened, I worked out the plan of attack that follows.

I beat the yips in about one month. You may do it quicker, or it may take a bit longer. But trust me, THIS WILL WORK.

How to Beat the Yips

First, I don't want you to "practice"—at least not in the normal sense of the word. Everybody knows how hard it is to take your game from the range to the course. I'd prefer that you avoid anything that resembles "practice" and just play golf, at least until you have this yips thing beaten. That way you'll always be putting under pressure, the actual conditions that brought on this yipping problem in the first place. For some of you this will be difficult, because your brain will insist that you can't possibly score using the method I'm going to teach you.

That's exactly what we want. Remember, your brain is attempting to over-control your putting, and we want to frustrate it until it simply gives up. This frustration is the key to beating the yips, so it's going to be uncomfortable. I'll be saying this over and over again, because a large part of your success depends on your understanding of this fact.

Mental frustration is the key to beating the yips.

Look, you developed the yips because your brain had a noble purpose—improving your putting. Unfortunately it pursued that goal in the only way it knew how—namely, over-analyzing and micromanaging your stroke. We're going to change your mental game by giving your brain what it wants—a way to improve your putting. The desire to improve your putting isn't the problem; the way your brain chose to do so is.

When we're done, your brain will have a new and clearer understanding of how to improve... but getting there is going to stretch your mind in a new way. As long as you understand this and don't give up, you *will* succeed.

Obviously, if you aren't going to practice, you're going to *play*. You read that right; we are going to solve this problem by actually playing golf rather than by standing on a practice green somewhere, mindlessly hitting putts and reinforcing the yipping mindset.

Kiss Your Yips Goodbye

In fact, you're going to continue to putt exactly the same way you always have—I doubt that anything was wrong with your original stroke, and I think that fixing it will give you more confidence in your putting ability than if we just change it. This will affect your confidence in two ways; you'll see that your original stroke could be trusted, and you'll realize you can improve your putting no matter how bad it may be. This knowledge can be a foundation for avoiding yips in the future.

It's time for you to beat the yips. To do it, you're going to continue to putt exactly the same way you always have... with one difference:

You're going to look at the hole and not the ball.

Now this is not a new drill. Pros and amateurs alike have practiced hitting balls while looking at the hole for a long time. However, we're going to make a slight change to it. You see, most people can see the hole *and* the ball when they do this drill.

You're not going to be able to see the ball. For all practical purposes, you'll be putting blind. All you'll be able to see is the hole.

Once you get past the initial shocked response of "I can't even hit the ball when I'm looking at it and you want to make it impossible for me to see the ball at all?!?!" you may think to ask, "Hmmmm... in that case, why don't I just close my eyes?"

That, my friend, is a very good question, and it's part of the key to beating the yips. Here's the reason: Although we don't want you to see the ball when you stroke it, *we do want you to see what the ball does after it's been struck*.

Remember, yips are an attempt to micromanage the stroke. When your brain *sees* the yipped putt behave badly, it reinforces the yip reflex because your mind becomes even more determined to control things better next time. The problem isn't the hole; the problem is that you are trying to hit the ball in far too precise a manner.

If you can't see the ball when you stroke it, you can't micromanage it; if you can't micromanage it, you can focus on how the stroke *feels*, as opposed to how it *looks*. That's your problem, isn't it? You're so caught up in technique that you can't just feel your stroke.

Granted, you could do that with your eyes closed. But if you can't see where the ball's going, how are you supposed to know if you struck the ball with

Ruthless Putting

proper speed and line? Ultimately, what you need is confidence—call it *faith*—that you can putt the ball with the proper line and speed, even if you don't strike the ball "absolutely perfectly."

Once your brain *sees* this unmanaged putt going where it's supposed to go, it will convince your brain that it no longer needs to micromanage your stroke. That will break the yip reflex so your brain "has permission" to swing smoothly again.

You'll need to spend a few moments on the practice green to adjust your setup in order to make this work. To keep from looking at the ball, you're going to turn your head toward the hole and close the eye closest to the *ball*. (That means the right eye for a rightie, the left eye for a leftie.) You continue to turn your head toward the hole until your nose blocks your open eye's view of the ball. You'll do this after you set up but before you stroke the putt.

> *Although we don't want you to see the ball when you stroke it, we **do** want you to see what the ball does after it's been struck.*

Setting up so that you can strike the ball along your aim line when you can't actually see the ball isn't that difficult; it usually just requires you to move the ball a bit forward in your stance. This is because turning your head toward the hole tends to move the contact point forward, which means you'll hit the ball early if it's at its normal position and push the putt. While you're learning where to place the ball, you can practice the simple routine we'll use to make the putt.

First, pick a reasonably straight putt on the practice green, maybe five or six feet long. (We don't want a long putt, but we do want it long enough to require a bit of feel and also long enough for us to watch.)

Next, set up normally with your ball in its normal position. Position the ball relative to your hands as normal, then close your eye, turn your head, and stroke the putt.

Kiss Your Yips Goodbye

Yes, you'll probably feel like an idiot. That's a normal response; your brain is losing control and it doesn't like that one bit. This is a good thing! Just imagine how hard you should stroke the putt... and then do it! Don't rush, but don't spend a lot of time either. This shouldn't take more than two or three seconds.

If you did what I just said, your ball probably went just about the right distance, and quite possibly on a straight line to the hole. You may be surprised, but you shouldn't be. If I gave you a ball and asked you to throw it to me underhand, you'd toss it to me and your distance and direction would probably be almost perfect... and you wouldn't look at either your hand or the ball before you threw it. If I moved to several different spots and asked you to throw it again, it would probably be almost perfect each time... and not once would you look at your hand or the ball. Using a putter just "makes your arm longer" and your brain will adjust quickly if you just give it a chance.

If the putt went in the hole, your setup is probably correct. Just set up normally for each putt during your round.

If the ball didn't go in the hole, we need to adjust your setup. The goal here isn't a textbook stroke; the goal is a *predictable* stroke. We can adjust both ball and foot position to get a wayward stroke on line. We're going to use them now to fine-tune your setup.

If you swing on an arc, foot position is merely a matter of comfort. Focus on ball position—move it back if you're pulling the putt, move it forward if you're pushing. Make your adjustments in one-inch increments; you probably won't need to move the ball more than an inch forward or backward from your normal setup to make this work. Making this adjustment is the trickiest part of this whole routine, simply because you can't place your hands over the ball. (Moving the ball and then placing your hands over the ball *will not* change the contact point.) Moving the ball *forward* in your stance means you must place your hands *behind* the ball; moving the ball *backward* in your stance means you must place your hands *ahead* of the ball. Got that?

Again, after you make an adjustment, try the "one-eyed putt" and note where the ball goes. Make adjustments until the ball goes straight toward the hole.

Ruthless Putting

If you swing straight forward and straight back (as a shrugger would), moving the ball forward or backward should only adjust how solidly you hit the ball. If your ball went left or right, you may need to adjust your foot position. If you pushed the putt, open your stance a little; if you pulled the putt, close your stance slightly.

After you make the adjustment, try the "one-eyed putt" again and see if the ball goes straight to the hole. If these adjustments don't straighten the path of the putt, there's a good chance you're stroke isn't a straight line after all. It's no big deal; just try changing the ball position—move it back if you're pulling, move it forward if you're pushing. Tinker with these two adjustments for a little bit and eventually you'll find a place where the putt goes straight.

When you discover the position that lets you stroke the ball in a fairly straight line, use that position for the remainder of your war against the yips. If you stick with it, that war won't last long.

These instructions should have worked for 90% or more of you. If they do, great; skip to the next section. If you continue to have difficulty getting the ball to go straight, even after trying all these adjustments, then this may help:

If you still can't get the ball to go straight, you probably have an unorthodox stroke where you hold the face open or closed through impact. If you've understood what this book says, you know there's nothing wrong with an unorthodox stroke that works. However, if you're yipping and also having trouble getting this "one-eyed stroke" to work, you may need to try something new.

I suggest rotating the club in your grip so you can make your normal stroke without adding a new manipulation to it. This may mean that, if your thumbs are normally on the flat part of the handle, you'll need to regrip so your thumbs are on the edge of the flat spot. Don't worry that it looks weird; you won't be able to see the new club orientation during the swing anyway!

Take It to the Course

Once you can hit the ball reasonably straight without being able to see the club actually hit the ball, you're ready to take this "new stroke" to the course.

Play your game as normal. Once you reach the green, go through your normal routines for reading greens and setup, so you can start the ball along your chosen line *using the new ball position you worked out earlier.* Close your eye and turn your head toward the hole so your nose blocks your view of the ball, just like before.

Now make the putt.

For some of you, this will be an excruciating process. Your brain will scream obscenities at you, call you an idiot, do all sorts of things to distract you from the simple act of putting. *Refuse to give in*. Concentrate on the putt and only the putt; stroke the ball just hard enough to make it die in the hole. Follow this procedure for every single putt, even the tap-ins.

Yes, you heard me right. *Even the tap-ins*.

The first few times you do this, your results might not be too good. This isn't because the stroke is flawed, but because you have to expend so much energy fighting yourself. But if you stick with it, in short order you'll notice that you're two-putting most of the time... and the second putt is a tap-in. Before long, some of the first putts will drop.

When I say "in short order" I'm not talking several weeks. I'm talking several *holes*. By the end of the first round you play this way, you should be absolutely shocked by how well you're putting. Your biggest challenge will be ignoring the whining you hear in your mind.

Enlightened Thinking

IF YOU MAINTAIN A RELAXED GRIP AND STROKE THE BALL WITH A GRAVITY SWING, IT IS VIRTUALLY IMPOSSIBLE TO YIP. What the process you have learned in this chapter does is make it easier to obey these two principles.

After all, if you can't see the ball, there's no reason to either tighten your grip (thereby violating Principle 3) or interfere with the pull of gravity.

What do we want to think about when we putt this way? I know I said "concentrate on the putt and only the putt," but what does that mean?

I want you to pay attention to how the putt *feels*. Remember how it felt when you swung the weighted string back in the tempo chapter? That's the sensation you're after. What we're doing is replacing the brain's obsession with mechanics; since you can't see where the ball is when you stroke it, your brain's unrealistic mechanical thoughts are useless.

Instead, we give it nothing more than a feeling, a rhythm, to focus on. Think back to what I said earlier

Ruthless Putting

about throwing a ball underhand. Try it; you don't look at the ball or your hand, but you feel something. What is that feeling? Does your putt feel anything like that?

Your brain will continue to try and take over the stroke but, if you don't look at the ball, it has nothing to grab onto but that feeling. And eventually, if you refuse to give in to the brain's complaints, if you continue to putt without looking at anything but the results of the putt, the brain will stop complaining and realize that *the feel is more reliable than its obsession with mechanics.*

Need another feel to help the brain focus? Before you putt, step to the edge of the green, hold the ball at shoulder height as if you were going to take a drop in the rough… and drop the ball. Try to feel the speed of the ball as it falls to the ground. How long does it take from the time you let go until it hits the ground? Imagine your downstroke begins when you let go, and that you

> ***I want you to pay attention to how the putt feels. Remember how it felt when you swung the weighted string back in the tempo chapter? That's the sensation you're after.***

contact the ball when it you hear it hit the ground. You'll find this is remarkably close to the actual rhythm of your stroke. Try to feel this speed when you putt.

Keep pointing out to your brain how your putting improves when you can't see the putt. "Wow, look how close that ball got to the hole… and I couldn't even see how the putter made contact with the ball. I don't get that close when my mechanics are perfect! My feel is much more accurate now…" Don't lie to yourself; your brain won't be fooled if you tell yourself things that aren't true. But this stroke will certainly feel better and smoother; reinforcing the positive things you see and feel when you putt will help your brain become re-educated.

How long will it take? That will vary. My yips were pretty bad but I was determined that I would not be beaten. Well into the third round I played this way, I noticed my brain wasn't giving me any problems, so I decided to see if I could putt normally. I set up, looking

Kiss Your Yips Goodbye

at the ball like usual... and yipped. I immediately went back to "one-eyed putting" and my brain quieted down again. After four rounds I was able to putt normally again without yips. I haven't had a problem since... because now I don't over-analyze my stroke.

Your results may vary, of course. But if it takes you ten or twenty rounds (or even more) to beat the yips, isn't it worth it? Psychologists say it takes roughly four weeks to change a habit (and I was playing only one round a week at the time); so it may be that the number of rounds you play isn't important, but rather your refusal to give in for the whole month.

Either way, one thing is for sure... yips *can* be beaten. If you are determined to beat them and you consistently use a well-thought-out method like this one, you *will* beat them. People learn new ways of doing things all the time, and beating yips is nothing more than re-education.

Here's a quick summary to make sure you understand the main points about beating yips:

- *Yips are simply an attempt to micromanage the putting stroke.*
- *To beat the yips, you have to frustrate your brain's attempts to analyze and manage every little aspect of the swing.*
- *To do this, you find a way to keep the brain from seeing the execution of the stroke while still seeing the results, thus forcing it to focus on the feel of the swing rather than the mechanics.*
- *You do this until the brain finally gives up on mechanical manipulation and embraces the feel of the stroke.*

Finally, let me explain one last time why this plan of attack works.

I'm not saying you don't want or need to understand the mechanics of your stroke; every golfer needs this knowledge in order to keep their stroke in working order. But you don't want to think about mechanics *during* your stroke; when you play this game, you want to play by *feel*. Ideally, you develop the stroke using sound mechanics, note how this stroke feels, then use that feel when you putt.

The problem is over-analyzing the mechanics. You want to view your mechanics with as little technical

Ruthless Putting

analysis as you can; you aren't trying to develop a perfect stroke. It's one thing to know your right elbow moves away from your side when you putt; it's another thing to know your right elbow moves three inches away from your side, then the right hand moves two inches past the elbow position before the right wrist flexes 30° past a line extending perpendicular from the ground.

Do you understand the difference? If you do, you may never be troubled by yips again.

Let's Review Your Arsenal Against the Yips

You have an entire arsenal of weapons to defend yourself against the yips, and you need never suffer from them again.

Let's review your options.

First of all, you now know what causes yips. Yips are the result of attempting to micromanage your swing. If you over-analyze your swing and try to make adjustments during your swing, that's the recipe for yips. Now that you know this, you can stop doing it and eliminate future yips problems.

You've learned the Basic Principles of Good Putting, especially Principle 3 (keep a relaxed grip). If your putting starts to go south, IMMEDIATELY CHECK YOUR GRIP PRESSURE. A too-tight grip is one of the major barriers to making a free stroke. My guess is that this is the first *physical* mistake a player makes on his way to Yipsville, so checking your obedience to this principle is your first line of defense against the yips.

You've also learned how to use a gravity swing to control your swing speed, so you've eliminated yet another of the major barriers to making a free swing. A gravity-powered swing is a feel on which you can safely concentrate, giving you a useful swing thought; and such a swing is remarkably consistent, providing increased confidence during the rough spots that invariably come. This knowledge is another useful defense against the yips.

You have four standard stroke styles (along with their blends and variations) so you can switch to a new stroke if you wish. Now you can tailor your existing swing to better suit you, or you can create an entirely new swing to take better advantage of your strengths and minimize your weaknesses.

And finally, you now have a technique for overcoming yips. If you want to change your stroke, you can; just focus on a relaxed grip and a gravity swing as you

Kiss Your Yips Goodbye

develop it. On the other hand, if you love your current stroke, *you can continue using it* and use the "one-eye" method to change your mindset when you putt. And make no mistake; it's your *mindset,* the way you approach putting and the unrealistic expectations you bring to the game, that sets you up to get the yips... and it's your mindset that can end the yips forever.

It's time we exorcised the yips for good. And good riddance to them!

14 Putting It All Together

Just how are you supposed to put all this knowledge together? How do you organize all this stuff—which I keep telling you is very low-maintenance—into a low-maintenance putting game? It's not much good if it takes forever to learn how to use it all, is it?

I've got a variety of simple pointers to share with you in this chapter, things that will enable you to start getting extra mileage from your game with very little extra effort.

The Ten Minute Pre-Game Warm-up

Ok, it's Saturday morning, and time to join your weekly foursome for another stimulating round of competition. You arise bright and early, have a leisurely breakfast, and arrive at the course 90 minutes early—plenty of time to warm up, hit a couple of buckets of balls, and just generally work out the kinks...

Oops, was I dreaming again? This is a book for weekend golfers, not pros! It's really more like this...

Ok, it's Saturday morning, and time to join your weekly foursome—well, it used to be weekly before the kids arrived. Now you're lucky if you four can get together once a month.

Anyway, you drag out of bed (little Johnny was up sick half the night) and realize you overslept. You grab a cup of coffee and a stale donut (the breakfast of champions!) and rush out the door. You arrive at the golf course, run to the clubhouse with your pull cart bouncing wildly behind you, and arrive at the desk with minutes to spare.

This is a good morning. You have ten whole minutes to warm up before this round.

Putting It All Together

This is the most likely scenario, isn't it? You have a few minutes to prepare (if you're lucky) and you're so stressed that you can't figure out where to start.

Relax... I'll give you a hand.

When you get to the practice green, take a few deep breaths and calm down. You can do quite a bit of preparation in ten minutes if you don't panic. Like everything else we've talked about in this book, it's all about knowledge; you just have to know where to focus your energies.

I know you want to whack some drives but, trust me, it's not worth the effort. Your body needs time to warm up for the full swing, and time is the one thing you *don't* have. Just figure on taking it easy the first two or three holes. We'll swing a bit slower, with lowered expectations; the ball won't go quite as far, but it will probably be in the fairway (or at least playable). We can live with that. By the third or fourth tee we'll be warmed up and able to swing normally.

We're going to spend these ten minutes working on our putting and short game.

Take out a 6- or 7-iron and take a few practice half swings. Just pick a target and line up, take the club back until your arms are parallel to the ground and your wrists are slightly cocked. Now make a slow fluid motion using the gravity swing, as if you were hitting a high soft pitch. (This is a short game shot, after all.) Don't rush—make 10 to 15 of these pitch shots. This will start the loosening-up process and help you regain the feel of the most important part of your swing—the action through the hitting area.

Again, just focus on feeling a fluid stress-free swing. When you step up on the first tee, your body will be relaxed and the only change you'll need to make is lengthening your swing. In the meantime, just try to enjoy the motion of swinging the club!

On to the Green...

Now let's move on to some putting practice. Let me give credit where credit is due—I got the idea for this from Dave Pelz. But I've added a few things to help you prepare more quickly.

Take two or three balls to the putting green and drop them beside one of the holes. Yes, you heard me right... *beside* the hole. Try to find a fairly level part of the green, where you can putt away from the hole without reaching any major slopes.

Ruthless Putting

No, that isn't a misprint. We're going to putt *away* from the hole. Humor me, ok? Here's the logic behind it:

All of us have a tendency, when practicing our putting stroke but not aiming at a particular target, to make a specific length backswing most of the time. For example, I tend to take a backswing of between 18 and 24 inches. When I shorten that swing, as if I was tapping in a short putt, I tend to make a stroke slightly less than 12 inches long. These stroke lengths are pretty consistent, so they're good strokes for me to use as a baseline for gauging green speed.

I choose one of the putts—I'd probably start with the shorter stroke—and make practice putts away from the hole. Why? Because I want to make a free stroke, without regard for a target, to *see how far the ball rolls when I stroke it*. To do this, I hit all three balls. I don't try to hit the ball the same distance with each stroke; rather, I just make *the same length stroke* on each putt, then I see where they end up. They should travel nearly the same distance and, since this is a flat putt, should be fairly representative of how fast the greens are.

Now I walk over to the three balls and putt them back toward the hole. I'm aiming at the hole (practicing my setup), but I'm not worried whether I make them or not. I just want to see if they go about the same distance. Remember, if the putts away from the hole went with the grain, the putts toward the hole will probably come up a bit short. The reverse is true if the "away" putts were into the grain. That's ok; I want to see how much difference there is between the two.

After doing this two or three times, I should have a good idea of how far my 12-inch stroke will go. Now I have a baseline for gauging how much to lengthen or shorten my stroke on short putts. I go through the same routine on a sloped putt; how far does this length stroke send the ball downhill? How far on an uphill putt? These will give me a decent feel for most of the shorter distance putts I'll face during my round.

And it's only taken a few minutes.

Then I follow the same routine with the longer stroke.

Most of your ten minutes has been used up now. If you have any time left, use it to make a couple of chip shots from good lies just off the green. All you want to do is feel the proper motion of a chip, and you choose good lies so you don't have to do anything fancy. These will put you in a good frame of mind for the round.

Putting It All Together

This routine shouldn't take more than ten minutes. If you have less time, just go as far into the routine as you can without rushing. The pitches at the beginning are important for relaxing your wrists and body, and the short putts are the minimum you'll need to post a decent score. As long as you get these in, you should be in good shape for a decent putting round.

Now, some people will scoff at a routine this short. But the more frequently you use it, the more comfortable you'll become with it... and putting is largely about comfort anyway. Knowing what to do and why to do it will help you gain that comfort so vital to playing well. It's the little things—like a good ten-minute warmup—that can make the difference.

Now let's figure out exactly how we're going to use this knowledge. How do we decide when to be aggressive in our putting, and when should we just settle for getting the ball close? You'll get a lot of different answers to this question, depending on who you ask.

For convenience I call these two mindsets "attack putting" and "lag putting," although that's probably not the best terminology. Most people equate these terms with the length of a putt, and I don't have any such limitation in mind. They're simply ways of thinking about putts you expect or don't expect to make.

Let's look at each mindset in turn.

Attack Putting

First off, attack putting is NOT aiming straight at the hole and ramming the ball against the back of the cup. That may work for some of you, but it's not what I'm talking about here.

Attack putting is about probability. You have a putt that you have a good chance to make if you put a decent stroke on it, regardless of the length of the putt, and attack putting is your strategy for giving yourself the best chance to do so.

This mindset takes several things into account:

- *The game and the situation*
- *The condition of the green*
- *The type of putt*
- *Your ability and frame of mind*

Let's look at each one separately, to see how they affect your mindset when putting.

Ruthless Putting

The game and the situation

You might say that match play and stroke play are the same, but different. In both you try to shoot the lowest score you can; however, scores have different meanings. If you make a 7 and your opponent a 3 in stroke play, you are 4 behind and may need several holes to get close again; in match play, you're only one down and can get back even on the next hole if you play well.

As a general rule, match play rewards aggression while stroke play rewards caution. The game affects your approach to putting.

The situation also affects your putting. A putt in match play that keeps you from going one down with one to go (also known as being "dormie") is different from the identical putt early in the match. In the first case, if you miss you'll have to struggle just to halve the match, while in the second case you'll have plenty of time to come back and grab an advantage.

> *Putting is largely about comfort anyway. Knowing what to do and why to do it will help you gain that comfort so vital to playing well.*

Likewise, consider a stroke play tournament where money or victory is on the line. Knowing that you need to make a putt to win, and that there is only one place on the green from which you might make that putt, can influence your shot into the green. You have to weigh the advantages of taking a risky shot in—and maybe winning the tournament—versus missing that shot, taking two or three extra strokes, and falling well down the leaderboard... which could cost you prize money.

So the game you play and the situation you face affect your strategy.

The condition of the greens

Rough bumpy greens demand a different approach from glassy smooth ones.

This could be due to weather. Remember how upset some pros were at the 2007 Tour Championship? The course had been baked during a long hot drought and

Putting It All Together

there were some bare spots. Players made putts from everywhere... but the greens were "stimped" at only 10 rather than 12 or 13. Some felt this made the course too easy; others couldn't adjust to the lower speed.

All because of the weather.

Then again, it may just be the nature of the course. Unless you play at an expensive club, the conditions may be rougher. Most of the public courses in my area run $20-$40 per round; at this (thankfully) low price, they can't afford the large greens crew that a big name course has. Sure, it's fun to play St. Andrews—but at $300 per round, how often can you afford it?

Conditions can also change *during* a round, rain and wind being primary examples.

So conditions have to be taken into account.

The type of putt

No matter what the condition of the green, a sharply breaking downhill putt must be played differently than a straight uphill putt against the grain. Failure to adjust to this simple reality will send your scores soaring.

Your ability and frame of mind

Finally, how's your distance control? Are you pushing or pulling putts today? Do you push or pull putts *all the time*? Do you freak out over a 3-foot sidehill downhiller? Is your partner so obnoxious that the only reason you haven't killed him is fear of a two-shot penalty?

Anything that affects your frame of mind, or any special problem (or strength) that your putting abilities present, must be taken into account as well.

How do you juggle these things? They affect all putts, and many times we should be attacking a long putt; but first let's focus on the short putts.

How short does a putt have to be before you consider it a short putt? That's part of what juggling these things tells us.

Bobby Jones seems to have decided that a short putt is no more than three feet. At least, that's the longest he speaks of in his article "Short Putts" (BJOG 94):

> "The mental attitude in which we approach a short putt has a lot to do with our success. When we walk up to a putt of ten or fifteen feet, we are usually intent upon holing it; we know we shan't

Ruthless Putting

feel badly if we miss, so our entire attention is devoted to the problem of getting the ball into the hole. But it is quite different when the putt is only a yard long. Then we know we ought to hole it easily, and yet we cannot fail to recognize the possibility of a miss. Instead of being determined to put the ball into the hole, we become consumed with the fear of failing to do so. Our determination, if we may call it such, is negative. We are trying not to miss the putt rather than to hole it."

That really sums up the problem with short putts, doesn't it? *We are trying not to miss the putt rather than hole it.* You might think of attack putting as not trying *not* to miss putts. In attack putting, we try to make the putt regardless of its length; in lag putting, we try to miss the hole as closely as possible.

Jones speaks briefly of how missing a short putt can really destroy a player's game—the entire game, from tee to green, as the player progressively puts more pressure on the rest of the game to make up for poor putting. And he also speaks of the challenge of deciding whether to strike the putt "delicately" or "firmly"... although he never really gives us an answer.

However, in a later piece he writes that he thinks "...the swinger is normally better on the long approach putts, while the hitter, if he is good, is likely to excel in holing out from distances of fifteen feet or less" (BJOG 96). Jones observes that the hitter, as he calls him, doesn't have good touch but can make up for some of it by knocking in a lot of four- to six-footers. He also notes that the problem with this stroke is a tendency to yank or jab putts off-line. (Sound familiar?)

Of course, I've been advocating what Jones calls swinging the club, which he says is the stroke for touch and range. Jones himself never altered his style for short putts—we know this from his film lessons—and he wasn't too shabby on the greens.

But these are valuable insights for the attack putter. Let's consider how Jones assessed these two approaches.

The hitter will tend to excel at putts of fifteen feet or less, and especially putts shorter than six feet. Straight putts, uphill putts, and putts that don't break a whole lot are his forte. In fact, any putt that can be made with speed is right down his alley; he can hold the line better than most.

Putting It All Together

He lacks some touch; it's safe to say that the hitter needs to be very careful when facing downhillers and sharply breaking sidehill putts. He'll also probably prefer slower greens; fast greens will amplify his misses. For the hitter, line is everything; speed will rarely be a problem!

By comparison, the swinger excels at putts longer than fifteen feet. When faced with a long or tricky putt, the swinger will be more likely to leave a tap-in if he doesn't actually sink the putt... a putt which will more likely trickle in from the side of the cup than drop in the center.

While in theory the swinger should be able to adjust to any type of green with equal ease—that is the nature of touch, after all—he will likely find slow greens more problematic than fast ones. A player who feels his way into the hole will have an easier time holding the line on a fast green; he may be uncomfortable striking the putt firmly enough to reach the hole on a slow green. For the swinger, distance control is everything.

If they miss, the hitter will likely be long and the swinger, short.

These tendencies affect the strategy of each when attack putting.

The hitter simply must get used to having three- or four-footers coming back if he is to make the most of his putting. Trying to get too cute with distance will destroy his game, since distance control is the weaker part of his game. Leaving the ball in a good position is also paramount, because his ball is less likely to feel its way into the cup. He needs to leave himself as many straight (or nearly straight) putts as possible.

The swinger, on the other hand, is probably going to leave a lot of putts short... but most of those putts will be tap-ins. He simply has to get used to this or it will destroy his confidence and his game. Swingers can try mental games to overcome this—aiming at a point a few inches behind the cup, for example—but being short will probably remain his natural tendency.

Lag Putting

I detest the concept of lag putting as "putting to a three-foot circle." Don't do it! Instead, focus on stopping the ball in that four-inch circle better known as the hole. Researchers know that your mind focuses on small targets better than big ones. Try to sink the putt.

Yes, you're going to miss of lot of those putts; it's ok to miss. As one of Rotella's books proclaims, golf is

Ruthless Putting

NOT a game of perfect. It's a *game*, period. Full stop. End of story. Don't try to solve personal issues with golf. (Personally, there have been many times in my life when I found the strength to deal with those issues simply because golf was *just* a game. It became a refuge, a place to escape to for a few hours and enjoy a world *without* pressure.) Learn to just enjoy striking putts to see how close you can get. It's not the end of the world if you three-putt, so don't convince yourself that it is. Skill at putting from a distance, like everything else in golf, will come to you if you learn to just enjoy the game.

Having said that, there's something else we can do to improve our long putting. In fact, it's so simple that I'm surprised that not even the greatest putters seem to have discovered it. At least they haven't mentioned it.

Well, maybe that's not quite true. On page 248 of his **Putting Bible**, Dave Pelz (who else?) spends three paragraphs on the idea that maybe we should consider carrying *two* putters, one for short putts and one for long putts. He gives the example of carrying a "broomstick" for short putts and a regular putter for the longer ones. (The "broomstick" would definitely help when you need two clublengths to take a drop!)

The problem I see with Dave's suggestion is that you have to develop two distinct putting styles—in his example, you have to learn his shrug stroke for the short putter and then learn the very different style required by the long putter—and that's going to take a lot of practice time. Still, he's on the right track.

Although what I'm about to say concerns what I've called your "attack putting" as well, I've put it in this section because I think most of us have more problems with long putts than short ones.

I mentioned earlier how Jones observed that there were two kinds of putters—he called them hitters and swingers—and that hitters seemed to excel at short putts while swingers were better from a distance.

Forget about "hitting" and "swinging" for a moment. Focus on the crux of the observation: "Long putting" and "short putting" each seem to favor a different stroke...

Have you considered developing two putting styles?

Whoa, now, don't look at me like that. I know I've based this whole book on the belief that weekend golfers have precious little time to practice putting, and I just said Pelz's suggestion required too much time. How in the devil do I expect you to find time to practice two different putting strokes?

Putting It All Together

Easy, big fella; hear me out.

I didn't say "two putting strokes"; I said "two putting *styles*." There's a world of difference in those two phrases. A new stroke has to be learned and practiced, but that ain't necessarily the case with a style. Suppose we could find a way to use the strokes we already know to help our putting? That's another matter entirely.

Imagination is imperative in the short game, and putting is part of the short game, isn't it? Let's see what kind of strokes we already have at our disposal, and then imagine some low-practice options to try.

First, we should determine whether we're better at long putts or short putts. We'll leave that stroke alone. Instead, we'll see what possibilities already exist that might help the weaker part of our putting.

I detest the concept of lag putting as "putting to a three-foot circle." Don't do it! Instead, focus on stopping the ball in that four-inch circle better known as the hole.

If Your Short Putting is Best...

Then you need to make some adjustments to your style of long putting. We've got a couple of options here.

(1) Develop a second stroke.

This isn't what you might think; you probably already have two different strokes. If you're a shrugger, popper, or twister, you already have a putting stroke that's different from your full stroke. In addition, you've probably focused on optimizing that stroke for shorter putts. Good! All you need to do is add a stroke for long putting; that way you can continue to focus your current putting style on those vital short putts. Since it will no longer be expected to do everything, I bet your short putting improves almost immediately.

As for that second stroke... your full game stroke probably looks remarkably like the hug or fold strokes. From a distance, using one of them with your putter may give you more feel for the distance. You can give it a try; you probably won't have to make any adjustments in the stroke at all beyond just taking a shorter swing.

Ruthless Putting

And don't panic about using your wrists too much; focus on making a gravity swing, and the ball will probably trundle right up to the hole just fine.

(2) Try putting with another club.

You say you're lousy at long putts? Well, there is absolutely no rule in golf that says you *have* to putt with a putter. Perhaps a longer club might solve your long putt woes.

Again, make no changes to your short putting style. But as the ball gets farther from the hole, go to a hybrid, a fairway wood, or even your driver. Personally I like the hybrid because it has a flatter face and a shorter shaft than the other two, but any of them should work. The idea here is to use your normal putting stroke with the longer club. This will entail a couple of minor changes.

First, if you're used to setting up with your eyes over the ball… well, it just ain't gonna happen. Don't let this worry you. You make most of your long shots with your eyes well inside the target line, so you're used to this. And since we're talking about long putts here, the line isn't as critical as the speed anyway. You'll be surprised just how good you'll be at picking a line, and you'll have less of a problem with that old bugaboo of falling so in love with the line that you forget to hit the ball.

Second, you'll probably need to alter your grip a bit to use this longer club. Basically, since the shaft is longer, you may need a grip that covers a longer stretch of the grip to better stabilize the club. I'd recommend a split-hand grip if your regular grip feels a little "floppy." Don't forget the possibility of a regular crosshand or a crosshand split grip either.

Finally, don't worry about the ball bouncing. A well-struck chip rolls really well; so will your well-struck putt—better in fact, because there's no long grass to get caught between the ball and the clubface.

I've got a couple of other suggestions, but they can work with short putting problems as well. I'll get to them shortly.

If Your Long Putting is Good…

Then you need help with your short putts. One possibility that should immediately jump to mind is…

(3) Grip down.

I bet when you have a short chip, you choke down on the grip more than when you have a long chip, don't you?

Putting It All Together

Try the same tactic with your putter. On your long putts hold the putter normally, but on the short ones grip *WAY* down, even placing one hand all the way down on the shaft if you need to. (Remember, only one hand needs to have a good grip on the club. When you don't need power, it doesn't take much of a grip to steady the club.)

The concept is simple: Think of your putter as a wedge; adjust your grip for different shots.

You say you're lousy at long putts? Well, there is absolutely no rule in golf that says you have to putt with a putter. Perhaps a longer club might solve your long putt woes.

Suggestions That Work with Both Problems

There are some solutions that, depending on what your regular putting style is, can work for either problem.

(4) Use two different grips.

Just holding your putter differently can change the way you putt. If you normally putt with, say, a reverse-overlap grip and it works well for long putts but not for short putts, try changing the grip you use for the short putts. Try a cross-hand grip or maybe a split-hand grip.

Just a personal observation: There are exceptions but, as a general rule, grips that keep the wrists fairly rigid, like the cross-hand grip, seem to work better for short putts. Grips that allow the wrists to flex, like the conventional grip, seem to favor long putts. It makes sense if you embrace the Jones idea that "hitters" are better on short putts and "swingers" are better on long putts. I don't know if Jones was right; but it does seem that line is a bit more important on short putts, and distance on long putts. Feel free to experiment a little.

(5) Change your stance.

Something as simple as changing your stance when faced by some of your more troublesome length putts can help you make more of them. You have three options here—open, closed, or square; don't be afraid to experiment a little.

Ruthless Putting

Changing your stance can affect not only your swing arc (think about the way Nicklaus putted), but it also affects how you see the line. This is why I think you may find this helpful; it should go without saying, but the ability to perceive line and distance accurately can make a huge difference on your ability to make putts.

(6) Putt "other-handed."

Don't throw this idea out until you've heard me through. It may surprise you.

Let's say your dominant hand (and I mean the one you use the most everyday, not necessarily when you play golf) is your right hand. I'm going to suggest you try putting "leftie" and change to a *right-hand-low* grip. Your "normal" hand will be in control of the club, but now you've gripped down a bit.

If your dominant hand is your left hand, go "rightie" and grip with the left hand low.

The basic principle here is to switch sides, then place the dominant hand low on the grip. I call this technique "playing other-handed." Essentially you're backhanding the putt, which is a fairly natural move—if you've ever hit a tennis backhand or thrown a Frisbee, you've already used this motion. Besides, it's not unusual for golfers to backhand short putts, even if their putter isn't built for it.

Obviously, this is a more expensive option than the others. Unless you normally use a two-sided blade putter, you're going to have to buy a second putter. Not only that, but you'll have to carry two putters in your bag, which means you'll have remove another club. But I agree with Dave Pelz here—I bet you've got at least one club in your bag that you never use or don't use well at all; if you can cut several shots from your game by replacing that club with a second putter… why not?

Before you decide to go this route, try this out at the pro shop's practice green—not once, but on at least three or four different days. That should be enough to let you know whether trying this option is worth your time… and money.

I know you think this is a bizarre idea and you're going to just skip over it. I'm begging you, DON'T! I have an old blade putter (the one used earlier in the pop putt experiments) and I wanted to try this technique myself before recommending it.

The results of my attempts were nothing short of *frightening*.

Putting It All Together

I spent maybe five minutes—no more—working on the stroke, and most of that was spent trying different ball positions, foot positions, and grips (I tried it with hands together and hands split). The beauty of trying is just how little practice it takes to get reasonably good; I spent most of this time searching for any "secret" that the technique might hold. When I first started, I pulled about half of my putts, but not badly; at 20 feet I was about four inches off line—about one cup width.

At the end of five minutes I was able to putt almost as well as I do normally. None of the variations seem to affect the accuracy, but I did tend to pull putts. (A quick note: you probably know that Phil Mickelson is right-handed but plays left-handed. I've noticed that when he misses putts, he tends to pull them too. I assume this a

*Let's say your dominant hand (and I mean the one you use the most everyday, not necessarily when you play golf) is your right hand. I'm going to suggest you try playing "leftie" and change to a **right-hand-low** grip. Your "normal" hand will be in control of the club, but now you've gripped down a bit.*

normal tendency with this style.) I suppose I was rolling my forearm during the stroke. Remember the original one-handed glass experiment back in chapter 3?

One thing I tried was extending my right index finger down the shaft, and gripping down enough that my index finger was on the metal. This gave me a much better feeling of control without having to tighten my grip.

I found that I needed to turn my right hand (my dominant hand) slightly to the left on the grip (this means I *strengthened* my right hand grip); the left hand remained in the normal parallel position. This is the Dave Stockton suggestion from the grip chapter. Once I did that, the ball rolled true most of the time. I also tried turning my right hand to the right (*weakening* it) and that seemed to work as well, although it felt a little weird.

The next time I tried this experiment, the results weren't quite as good. I continued to have some

Ruthless Putting

problems with pulling putts, despite turning my hand slightly. I have tried this putting style several times since and have concluded that the problem was a failure to get my hands over the ball, tilting the club slightly toward the hole as I suggested many chapters ago. This is a problem I sometimes have when putting crosshanded, so it's not a surprise that it showed up here as well. (Note to crosshanded putters: If you're having a problem with your line, check to be sure your hands are over or slightly ahead of the ball. That may mean moving the ball back a bit in your stance; that's what I had to do with this stroke to clear up the problem.)

I expected that putting "other-handed" would be a fairly easy stroke to learn, but I was shocked that it was *so* easy. If I were having problems with my putting, I would certainly consider buying a left-handed putter. The results from this test were just too good to ignore.

They also made me wonder if Phil Mickelson's putting prowess comes from so much practice... or if it's just as much because he's a right-hander who putts other-handed?

It's worth thinking about...

Change Your Mindset

That's six different ideas you can try to improve the weak areas of your putting. I think the most underrated technique is simply using different styles for short and long putts; you can see the pros use most of the others pretty regularly. (Although they generally use hybrids and woods only when putting from off the edge of the green.)

You have plenty of options; all you need to do is change your mindset. Anybody can learn to putt well, and it doesn't take hours and hours of practice. (Are you tired of hearing me say that? I'm not tired of saying it.) But you've got to find how *you* putt best, and that means you've got to get past the common beliefs people hold about putting... and stop worrying about what people might think if you adopt an unusual style.

Engrave this truth on your mind... and on top of your putter too if necessary: There may be an *accepted* way to putt; there may even be a *desirable* way to putt. But there is no single correct way to putt. Don't let other people's expectations keep you from playing your best game.

And don't let anyone convince you that a good plan of attack has to be complicated. A simple warmup routine, the ability to recognize when a putt requires caution, and an imaginative approach to overcoming putting weaknesses can give you a serious advantage on the greens.

From Off the Green

And one last thought before I go:

You probably putt from off the green quite often. There's nothing wrong with that but, as I said in the last section, a good putting stroke can be used with other clubs besides the putter.

The pros do it all the time... so why don't you?

Using other clubs can give your putting stroke some extra range, allowing you to utilize its best qualities from spots where a putter simply can't go.

The rule of thumb is simply not to use your putter unless the grass is very short—what some players call a "tight lie." This rule varies a bit with different types of grasses; it all depends on how far "down" your ball sits. If the grass is stiff enough to keep the ball up on top, you may be able to "putt" from taller grass.

Don't use the shorter irons with your putting stroke unless you're very close to the green and the hole. I

> *The rule of thumb is simply not to use your putter unless the grass is very short—what some players call a "tight lie."*

know this goes against much of what you've heard—most pros and teachers will tell you to get the ball on the ground as soon as possible when you chip—but that's with a normal chipping stroke. Your putting stroke isn't as powerful and doesn't hit down on the ball as much as a chipping stroke, so the ball won't get as high or fly as far as you expect.

Your best results will come with the longer clubs, especially your hybrids. I find my 3-iron hybrid works very well; 3-woods and even drivers work well, but shaft length can be a problem. Don't worry about getting your eyes over the line of the putt; just pretend you're striking a very, very short drive! Pick a spot to hit the ball over, then line up parallel to the "line of flight" and make your putting stroke; it'll work just fine.

Ruthless Putting

Don't attempt to hit down on the ball; a putting stroke is a sweeping stroke, even when used from off the green. Position the ball normally; if you can't get the club on it cleanly that way... **don't putt.** In fact, if you're positioning your hands over or ahead of the ball when you putt normally, the extra loft of your irons and woods should give you pretty decent contact; you may even be able to move the ball a bit more forward in your stance. Just don't risk leaving the ball in the rough. The reason for using a putting stroke is to improve your odds of getting the ball close, and you're defeating the purpose if you just make the shot harder.

Be sure to practice using your putting stroke for this "mini-chipping" motion before you actually use it on the course. It won't take much practice to learn what you can and can't do. That's the real beauty of putting, after all... even a child can do it.

And now we come to the end of the book. If you've taken the time to understand the principles in this book, and if you're willing to try some new techniques, then you're well on your way to becoming a ruthless putter. It won't be long before **you** are the one everybody tries to copy.

Ruthlessness is its own reward. Where you go from here is up to you.

Appendix:

Troubleshooting with the Basic Principles

To paraphrase the comedian, "Death is easy. Putting is hard." At least, that's what most people seem to believe.

It's not true, of course. That smooth stroke we developed in the gravity chapter is a breeze to use, a simple swing with which we can easily send that disobedient little sphere to its final resting place. (The bottom of the hole, that is!)

But occasionally our stroke can get a little out of whack. Usually it's just a simple matter of poor setup or incorrectly adjusted equipment; so the purpose of this appendix is to help you to quickly identify the problem and get it back on track with a minimum of effort.

The Seven Principles of Good Putting not only serve as a good foundation from which to build a low-maintenance swing built on our own individual stroke, but also as the basis of a simple maintenance checklist. First we'll break down each principle by its potential problem areas. There is no particular importance to the order in which the problems are listed.

You'll notice is that some problems affect more than one principle. For this reason I've included a list of those problems in alphabetical order, so you can find them more quickly. If you're having difficulty with two or more principles and see the same problem listed under all of them, by all means check that problem first.

Finally, you'll find an explanation of each problem, also listed in alphabetical order.

Ruthless Putting

There's an additional setup problem not directly addressed by the principles: difficulty seeing the line of the putt. Don't confuse this with reading greens, which was covered in chapter 11; here we're talking about seeing the line you've already chosen *once you're standing over the ball*. Most teachers prefer to get the eyes over or just inside the line of the putt. (Jones never says, but the video lesson seems to show his eyes well inside his line of aim.) At any rate, the problem is called "ocular dominance" and is covered in the last entry, "vision problems."

A Troubleshooting Guide to the Seven Principles

1) The putterface should remain square to the stroke path; the forearms should NOT rotate during the execution of the stroke.

Hands too close together; incorrectly-sized handle; poor ball position; face angle needs adjustment; handle crooked; grip crooked; Principle 4 violated.

2) The putter should be held in a "parallel" grip, where both palms are parallel to the face of the putter and the back of the forward hand faces the target.

Handle crooked; grip crooked; face angle needs adjustment.

3) The putter should be held lightly, without tension in the arms or shoulders or hands.

Unnatural position or posture; incorrectly-sized handle.

4) The putter handle should be held so that the shaft aligns with the forearms.

Handle too much in fingers.

5) The putter should never follow an outside-to-inside path (a cut stroke).

Incorrect alignment; poor ball position; not enough arm swing.

6) The putterhead should travel on a long low path, as close to the ground as possible, both going back and through.

Conscious use of wrists (too much/too soon); not enough arm swing; poor weight distribution.

Appendix: Troubleshooting with the Basic Principles

7) The lower body should not be rigid, neither should it be consciously moved. It should move no more than the natural execution of the stroke requires.

Unnatural position or posture; head movement; stance too wide/narrow.

An Overview of the Problems...

(* indicates an equipment adjustment)
- a) Conscious use of wrists (too much/too soon).
- b) Face angle needs adjustment.*
- c) Grip crooked.
- d) Handle crooked.*
- e) Handle too much in fingers.
- f) Hands too close together.
- g) Head movement.
- h) Incorrect alignment.
- i) Incorrectly-sized handle.*
- j) Not enough arm swing.
- k) Poor ball position.
- l) Poor weight distribution.
- m) Stance too wide/too narrow.
- n) Unnatural position or posture.
- o) Vision problems.

...and the Problems Themselves

a) Conscious use of wrists (too much/too soon).

Learning to use gravity in a swing is easy. Learning to *trust* that swing is often more difficult. For reasons we discussed in the yips section, the need to control the ball by hitting it can be almost irresistible.

The result is a wristy swing, and it can take two forms. The wrists can cock too much, exaggerating the normal motion made by the wrists. Or the wrists cock too soon, moving much earlier in the swing than they would if allowed to flex naturally. In either case, the club no longer depends on gravity for its tempo, but on the small muscles of the hands and forearms.

There's a difference between a swing where relaxed wrists "just happen" to move a bit as the club swings and one where the wrists are consciously used in an attempt to duplicate that move. While this can affect distance control because it's hard to consistently control the power these muscles produce, it can also result in "lifting" the clubhead on the backswing. Instead of swinging back low and coming through low, the head

Ruthless Putting

moves upward abruptly on the backswing, and the downswing becomes more of a chop down on the ball. Result? The ball hops in the air, which can affect both distance and direction control.

Spending a little more time with the weighted string can help here. It's hard to swing that string when you consciously use the wrists.

b) Face angle needs adjustment.*

When you grip the handle with a parallel grip but the face of the club still isn't parallel to the palms, the ball will not go where it's aimed even if you make a perfect stroke. Problems *b*, *c*, and *d* represent three different causes for this problem.

In this first cause, the clubhead is actually out of alignment with the shaft. This was discussed in more detail in the chapter on equipment; here I'll just point out that this has to be fixed by a golf club repairman.

c) Grip crooked.

Sometimes you make a proper parallel grip but your hands are turned on the handle. By this I mean that, if you hold the club up in front of you so that the toe of the club is perpendicular to the floor (what you might call a "12 o'clock position"), both of your thumbs may point toward 1 o'clock, or 11 o'clock, or some other "time."

If your grip is twisted on the handle this way, you may not realize it if you're using a round handle (like the ones on your irons and woods). The obvious solution in this case is to straighten out your grip—hold the club up with the toe at 12 o'clock and change your grip until the palms also point at 12 o'clock.

If you're using a flat-sided putter handle and your grip is twisted, your grip won't—and shouldn't—feel quite right. In that case, your solution will be the same as above. But if your grip *does* feel ok, you probably have the next problem.

d) Handle crooked.*

If you hold the club up in front of you so the toe of the putter points straight up, the flat side of a putter handle should also point straight up. This way, when you take a parallel grip, the thumbs will automatically be lined up down the center of the shaft and the palms will be parallel to the face.

Appendix: Troubleshooting with the Basic Principles

When the handle is crooked, the flat side points to the left or right rather than being centered. This causes the club face to point either left or right even when you swing properly. Needless to say, the ball won't go where you think you're aiming.

The solution is to have a new handle put on... and ask the club repairman to make sure it's on straight.

e) Handle too much in fingers.

When you hold the handle down in your fingers rather than along the lifelines of your palms, there can be a tendency to rotate the shaft like a doorknob as you swing. As you'll remember, Bobby Jones held the club down in his fingers and, as a result, had to resort to an unusual position for his left elbow to keep from unintentionally turning the clubface.

The obvious solution is to move the shaft up into the palms. However, if you absolutely must hold the club in your fingers (and who am I to tell you can't?), you can probably prevent the clubface from rotating by pointing your left elbow toward the hole. It worked for Jones, so it's worth a try.

f) Hands too close together.

This may sound like a strange problem, but hear me out.

If you turn a screwdriver with both hands, the wrists allow the hands to turn as a unit because they're very close together. By comparison, if you use a long wrench with one hand holding the head of the wrench on the nut and the other several inches down the handle, twisting your wrists won't loosen the nut; you have to move your *arms* to get the nut to turn.

Separating the hands helps take the wrists and forearms out of the stroke. If this is your problem, the easiest way to do this is to try a split-hand grip.

g) Head movement.

Have you got a problem with your head moving when you putt? Haven't been able to stop it?

Bet you have a wide steady stance, don't you? Or maybe you have a narrow stance and have to work really hard to keep your lower body still. Regardless of which one describes you, the result is the same: excessive head movement.

Here's how it works. It's a basic law of physics: *For each and every action, there is an equal and opposite reaction.*

Let's say you throw a punch with your right hand, and it finishes with your arm straight out at shoulder height. Your left shoulder moved back, didn't it? Here you see that basic law at work. It's especially noticeable with rotary body movements around your spine.

Now try it again, but stand with your left shoulder against a door jamb so it can't move backward. When you throw that punch this time I bet you get an unpleasant jerk as your head lurches forward. Why? The rotary motion of the shoulders was blocked, so your body lurched forward to let your left shoulder get into the position it would have if it had been able to move freely.

Or, to put it more simply, the forward action of the punch demanded a reaction by the opposite shoulder. If that action was blocked, the energy had to go somewhere... so it shoved your body forward.

OK, now think about your putting stroke. *Both* shoulders move in a rotary motion, in unison. Hmmm... something's got to move in the opposite direction. The most logical reaction would be a slight rotary motion in the hips or knees... but you've immobilized them, haven't you? What do you think happens?

Right. The hips try to rotate but, just like your shoulder against the door jamb, it has nowhere to go. So it shoves your spine in the opposite direction...

And your head and shoulders move toward the target.

The solution isn't to stiffen up more but to relax the lower body enough that it can flex. When you swing, the shoulders may not move much... neither will your lower body. But that tiny movement is vital to your balance during the stroke.

To test this, if your head is moving, try taking your stance with both feet together. This will easily allow a slight lower body movement. Then make some practice putts. If this solves the problem, you need to relax that lower body. Try a narrower stance, keeping the outsides of your feet no more than shoulder-width apart.

h) Incorrect alignment.

I think most people have some sort of alignment problem. The real complication here is that most teachers emphasize what I call an ideal setup, one where lines

Appendix: Troubleshooting with the Basic Principles

drawn through your ankles, knees, hips, forearms, and shoulders all line up parallel to your line of aim. Ideally, this should enable you to strike the ball squarely down that line time after time.

It's a complication because most people don't have ideal bodies. Because of this, I don't think most people are physically capable of using the ideal setup; everybody needs a few compensations to make consistent contact with the ball.

Most of the time, you should set your shoulders parallel to your aimline; but this is easier said than done since the hands are placed one below the other on the handle. Because of this, the shoulders *tilt*. This tilt is one reason the hug stroke is rarely used as a pure stroke; with the shoulders at different heights, their rotation around the spine isn't as simple a move as the theory suggests. I suspect it also explains the popularity of the pop stroke throughout history; popping requires less shoulder movement than any other style. Furthermore, it helps explain why the shrug stroke has become so popular; if you set up properly, the plane of shoulder rotation remains nearly perpendicular to the spine, eliminating both muscular strain and compensations for shoulder tilt.

At any rate, this is where open and closed stances come into play. If misused, they can result in some bizarre putting postures and bad alignment; but used properly, they can help compensate for the variations in the human body as well as the uneven position of the shoulders.

I'm a great believer in open and closed stances. It's part of what I call the Law of Extremes—a move is always more consistent if, instead of being in the center of a range of movement, it lingers near the extremes. Think of it this way: If you stand in the middle of a room and wave your arm around, you can move it to the left or the right. Move over to a wall and put your right shoulder against it, you can still move to the left—away from the wall—but you can no longer move to the right because the wall is in the way.

Opened and closed stances work the same way; they limit your ability to move in one direction while allowing freedom to move in the other direction. You can use this limitation to your advantage.

The open stance is the most typical variation from the ideal setup, and the reason why should be pretty clear.

Ruthless Putting

Unless you're using a crosshand grip, the open stance moves the lower shoulder ever-so-slightly closer to the line of the putt, making it possible to swing the putter back in an arc so narrow that it can almost match the shrug.

For putters in general and shruggers particularly, the pressure to stroke a putt straight can be unbearable. The quest for the perfect stroke is alive and well...

To those of you struggling to relieve the pressure (and that includes most of us), I offer a bit of heretical advice: Opening or closing your stance slightly can straighten out that stroke. I know, I know, that's not the way it's supposed to be done. But I ask you, which do you prefer—a textbook setup and hours of practice in an attempt to swing the club straight back (and a constant struggle if this is not a natural move for you), or a slight adjustment in foot position to make the best use of your natural tendencies?

Don't confuse this advice with what happens in a full swing. In a full swing you set your shoulders along the line of your feet; you continue to aim the clubface at the hole but change the swingpath to impart sidespin to the ball. If you aim your shoulders at the hole but change your foot position, you still end up moving along the line of your feet because of your hip movement through the swing. Either way, this isn't what we want in a putt—putts don't hook or slice, they just get pushed or pulled off-line.

In the much shorter putting stroke, there isn't enough movement in the hips to alter the stroke path. Instead, we're harnessing muscle tension to gently change the path. In the last section I told you how the laws of physics can cause your head to move, as the twisting motion around your spine pushes against an immoveable lower body. In this case, we still leave the lower body flexible; we're just changing the angle of the rotation. This is simpler than trying to adjust the entire setup; it's like using a fine adjustment screw. If you try to straighten out the line by changing the entire setup, you move your body a lot; turning the lower body only is a much more forgiving move, making the change while leaving some leeway for error.

Again, let me stress that you want to feel that your shoulderline is aligned with the aimline of the putt (unless you're using the modified pop setup). Move only your lower body; your foot position won't have to be exactly the same each time to get the same result, as long as it's close.

Appendix: Troubleshooting with the Basic Principles

i) Incorrectly-sized handle.*

When K.J. Choi began playing so well in 2007, winning both Jack and Tiger's tournaments, his putter drew a great deal of attention. It seems K.J. had installed a monstrously huge handle on his club... and was putting lights-out with it.

Although K.J.'s handle is larger than most, the theory has been around for a long time (at least, concerning the full swing). Ask any good clubfitter about handle sizing, and they'll tell you that using a smaller-than-normal handle will encourage a hook and a larger-than-normal handle encourages a slice. The reason? We tend to grip smaller handles more in the fingers, which encourages more rotary wrist movement (we discussed this in *e* above). Likewise, we tend to grip a larger handle more in the palms, which discourages rotary wrist movement.

And that's just what we want when we putt.

Short of buying one of those monster handles like K.J. uses (and I've noticed more pros are using them since K.J. has had so much success), you have two other options. You can get large flat-sided handles in a variety of sizes, and you can use regular or jumbo round handles on your putter. Your local pro shop should have several choices on hand, and changing the handle shouldn't take more than a few minutes. One of my older putters has a jumbo handle on it, and I enjoy using it a lot.

j) Not enough arm swing.

This problem is very similar to *a*—the conscious use of the wrists—but it has a slightly different effect. The wristy putter lifts the club very early in the stroke and effectively chops down on the ball. That's a parody of a true swing, but it uses muscle power to imitate wrist flex.

This problem is also a parody of a true swing, but it uses *speed* to create wrist cock. *The swing is short and quick* (that's why this problem is labeled "not enough arm swing"), causing the wrists to snap back sharply at the end of the backswing. Depending on the player's timing, the putter may not uncock in time to strike the ball, resulting in poor contact; or it may uncock rapidly, sending the ball zipping past the hole.

If your stroke is a true swing, it will be slower and will force you to make a longer backswing. A few minutes using the weighted string will help you correct this problem. Remember, while it's easy to learn how to swing, learning to *trust* that swinging motion takes time.

k) Poor ball position.

Everybody wants to know where to place the ball in their stance... but that's the wrong question to ask.

The right question is "Where are your hands?"

Your hands are your only contact with the club. (How many times have you heard that?) Yet have you considered how you're going to bring that club into contact with the ball? Let's think this through.

As you know by now, I like to let my arms hang straight down, then position myself so the ball is under my hands. This way, even if my stance varies somewhat from day to day, both my ball position and contact point remain consistent.

But not all of you will want the ball under your hands. You have three more possible positions you can use:

- ***Place your hands in front of the ball.*** *For example, when I place my hands directly over the ball, the shaft of the putter leans slightly forward. Natalie Gulbis places her hands considerably farther forward, and the shaft leans forward that much more.*
- ***Place your hands in line with the shaft.*** *The shaft is held vertically, perpendicular to the ground, and of course the hands are directly in line with it. Typically, this means the ball is placed just in front of the face of the putter.*
- ***Place your hands behind the clubhead.*** *This option isn't usually recommended, but Zach Johnson uses it and he hasn't done too badly. Obviously, the ball will be considerably ahead of the hands in this case but, as long as the club has been properly adjusted for this setup, it shouldn't be a problem.*

A quick note regarding these hand positions: Although you'll probably see most pros use the second one, the other two positions are actually provide more stable wrist positions. Since one wrist will be held in a bowed position throughout the stroke, the notorious "wrist breakdown" scenario never happens. With Position 2, it's easy to get too much wrist flex on the way back, and then get too much flex on the followthrough.

The point here is that ball position is dependent on where you place your hands. If your setup places your hands in front of your right thigh, this necessitates a ball position much farther forward than it would if your

Appendix: Troubleshooting with the Basic Principles

hands are held at the midpoint of your body. Where your hands are in relation to your *body* is determined by the grip you have chosen, the style of stroke you use, and how you stand when you address the ball. And where your hands are relative to the *ball* affects the adjustments that should be made to your putter, which are discussed in the equipment chapter.

So the answer to the question, "Where do I place the ball in my stance?" is "I should place the ball where my hands can best bring the club into contact with it."

l) Poor weight distribution.

Should you set up with your weight evenly distributed on both feet, or should you set your weight on your forward foot? The simple answer here is... do what feels good. Some setups make this choice for you, as when a shrugger sets up with their head *behind* the ball. In this case, the weight will be more on the *rear* foot... and that's ok.

The key here is stability. You should feel naturally balanced, not wobbly. You're not trying to immobilize your lower body. (I know I'm running this into the ground, but it's a major fault in most setups.) Do you feel unstable when you're just standing and talking to a friend? Probably not, but you aren't stiff and immobile either. This relaxed stability is the feeling you want.

m) Stance too wide/too narrow.

Stan Utley agrees with Bobby Jones when it comes to the stance. He like the feet spaced shoulder-width or less apart. Understand, when these two guys talk shoulder-width, they're measuring from the *outside* of the feet, not the inside as Dave Pelz does. That wider stance immobilizes the lower body, which is in keeping with Dave's attempts to establish a very straight back-and-through swing. Personally, I don't have a problem with body movement even if I shrug with a narrow stance. If you feel the need for stability, by all means take a wide stance. Nowhere is it written that there's only one way to putt. After all, that's the whole point of this book—finding your own putting style.

But for those of you who have been locked in an uncomfortable position just because you were told to, I now say to you (in my best Bible-Belt-tele-evangelist accent), "Ah free yew from this demon. Be healed!"

Ruthless Putting

n) Unnatural position or posture.

This problem is self-explanatory. If your setup feels strained or unnatural, it's extremely difficult to remain relaxed.

Several things can contribute to this problem, like putting your weight too much on your toes or your heels, bending over too much or standing too tall, twisting your body, or holding your arms in an awkward position. Regardless of what you've been told, Jones's advice to do things in the simplest way possible should be your guiding principle here; setup should feel as natural as you can make it.

The solution is self-explanatory as well: If your setup is a problem, CHANGE IT!

o) Vision problems.

I suspect that alignment causes so much trouble because of vision problems. Standing to the side of your aimline, it can be difficult to see straight down the line. What do you do? You contort your body into whatever position allows you to see that line clearly. As a result, you can see the line but your body is no longer aimed to stroke along that line.

Part of this solution concerns ball position. We've mentioned ball position relative to the hands, which affects your ability to start the ball on your chosen line, but ball position relative to the eyes determines your ability to *see* the chosen line.

The subject of eye position is complicated by the concept of *eye dominance*—simply put, you aim more with one eye than the other. Estimates put anywhere from 70-90% of the population in the "right-eye dominant" camp, with the remainder being "left-eye dominant." I've also seen figures indicating that as much as 15% of the population is equally dominant in both eyes.

Why is this important? Assuming the centers of your eyes are two inches apart and the player is right-handed, placing the ball directly under your nose means the right-eye dominant player is aiming from *behind* the ball and the left-eye dominant player is aiming from *in front* of the ball.

Clearly, this can cause some problems.

Discovering which of your eyes is dominant is pretty simple. According to the following Wikipedia web page:

http://en.wikipedia.org/wiki/Ocular_dominance

Appendix: Troubleshooting with the Basic Principles

there are at least ten different ways to test for it. Here's one way to do it, based on instructions you can find at:

http://www.archeryweb.com/archery/eyedom.htm

Holding both hands out in front of you, make a small triangle between your thumbs and the first knuckles of your index fingers. The triangle should measure a little less than an inch on each side.

With both eyes open, pick an object a few feet away from you and center it in the triangle.

Now, close your left eye. If the object is still visible, that's your dominant eye; if you can't see it anymore, the right eye is your dominant eye.

You can doublecheck your results by doing the test again but closing the right eye.

(I think dominant eye tests are always a little subjective, which means you can unintentionally "fudge" the results. And results can change over time; I used to test consistently left-eye dominant, but now get mixed results. There are exercises you can do to help strengthen the non-dominant eye; I heard that Michelle Wie used some special glasses to help her do it, but you can do the same thing with an eye patch. You can find more info by searching for "eye dominance test" or "cross dominance.")

Some people try to get their heads behind the ball when they putt; Phil Mickelson appears to do this. Dr. Joe Parent notes that the amount of offset a club has can affect some people's aim. (Offset was explained in the equipment chapter.) Glasses help some people, and open or closed stances can change the way you see the line as well.

I wish there was a simple solution to vision problems, but there isn't. How you see the line is something unique to you, and the best I can do is make you aware of some of the factors that affect your aim. But if you use the information in this chapter to eliminate the setup problems that violate the Seven Principles and thus make it more difficult to start the ball on the correct line, you should have less of a problem finding a way to see that line clearly.

A Final Thought: Setup is a Dirty Word

I really think we should change the term "setup" to something less... stiff. In an ideal setup we would just walk up to the ball and putt it, without any tension at all.

Ruthless Putting

That should be your guiding principle; the less pretense there is in your setup, the better you'll putt.

I like this mental approach: *The ball is an old friend I haven't seen in a while. I just want to walk up and shake his hand.* Think about this for a moment. Would you walk up to your friend, stop, take several seconds to place your feet properly, and wiggle your hands to loosen them up first? Would you reach out and take your friend's hand, then stand there motionless for several seconds before slowly and deliberately moving his hand up and down? Of course not! That would be an awful parody of a handshake, and your friend would look at you as if you were, shall we say... "socially inept." (If your friend was like mine, his description would probably be much more colorful!)

No, you'd just walk up, smile, grab your friend's hand, and pump it like there's no tomorrow. (Well, you would if you were excited to see him.) Imagine your friend greeted you this way. This casual approach would make you feel really good, wouldn't it? What else would you feel?

Warm. Confident. Relaxed. Pick your own adjective, but I bet they all describe feelings you want to have when you stand over a putt.

When you don't have lots of time to practice, it only makes sense to make your setup as relaxed and natural as possible. In fact, if you can eliminate the entire concept of "setup" from your game, you'll probably make a quantum leap in your scoring ability.

END

Buying this book entitles you to a FREE *Ruthless Chipping* EBOOK!

Ruthless Putting is available as an ebook at:

http://ruthlessputting.com

and readers who bought the ebook version also got a free ebook called *Ruthless Chipping,* which teaches you how to turn your low-maintenance putting stroke into a full-blown low-maintenance chipping stroke.

    Well, fair is fair. You bought a paperback version, *so you can get the free ebook also!* Just go to:

http://ruthlessputting.com/pbook/free

and follow the instructions.

www.ingramcontent.com/pod-product-compliance
Lightning Source LLC
Chambersburg PA
CBHW051212290426
44109CB00021B/2424